THE
CONVERSATION
GUIDE

THE CONVERSATION GUIDE

HOW TO SKILLFULLY COMMUNICATE, SET BOUNDARIES, AND BE UNDERSTOOD

J. L. Prevost, MCP, RCC

The Conversation Guide: How to skillfully communicate, set boundaries, and be understood.
J.L. Prevost, MCP, RCC

This book is intended to help people communicate and is not a substitute for therapy. The skills herein are designed to help you feel understood and to better understand others; they are not meant for manipulation or self-serving purposes.

Unless otherwise referenced, the information presented in this book comprises the author's own knowledge, theories, experiences, and opinions. In stories and examples, all names have been changed.

Please note that the content of this book may stir up overwhelming feelings or discomfort, and may cause changes in relationships. Contact first responders or a mental health professional if you ever feel unsafe.

Cover and interior design by Richard Ljoenes Design LLC.

ISBN (Paperback): 978-1-7777583-0-1
ISBN (Ebook): 978-1-7777583-1-8

Scintilla Therapy
Surrey, B.C., Canada

www.TheConversationGuide.com
First edition

To my clients

CONTENTS

PART II

HAVING DIFFICULT
CONVERSATIONS SKILLFULLY 137

PREFACE

DO YOU KNOW YOU NEED TO HAVE A DIFFICULT CONVERSATION but don't know how to start or are afraid the conversation will get derailed? Are you unsure of how to set boundaries effectively? Do you often feel misunderstood? As a counselor and therapist, I consistently see these issues arise with clients who need to communicate something important but don't feel they have the tools to do so. Seeing this need for conversation guidance, I created a set of skills to help people learn to better communicate and structure conversations.

The skills in this book came from many places: my experiences helping my clients, my own life, and my counseling training. In addition, you will notice references to Cognitive Behavior Therapy (CBT)[1] and Dialectical Behavior Therapy (DBT).[2] These forms of therapy, as well as my time working for a crisis hotline, interactions with my colleagues, and specialized knowledge from the counseling community, round out the skills I'll teach you in the pages that follow. (I'm forever thankful for the knowledge shared!) If you'd like more information about the sources of various pieces of content, a Recommended Resources is provided at the back of the book.

My goal is to give you tangible, stepwise instructions and skills for difficult conversations that are applicable to each and every situation you find yourself in. Armed with these skills, you'll gain the confidence to have any conversation you need—which will improve your relationships and, hopefully, improve your life overall!

—J. L. Prevost

INTRODUCTION

BREAKING UP WITH SOMEONE. SAYING NO TO YOUR FRIEND'S last-minute request. Setting a boundary with a family member. Asking your partner to do their part to clean up your shared space. These are just a few examples of difficult and emotionally intense conversations that we often put off. We avoid confronting and talking about these situations because we don't feel confident in our ability to start the conversation, handle our emotions, manage other people's reactions, not get defensive, keep the conversation on track, stay away from past cycles, and know when to wrap up the conversation.

This book is divided into two parts. Part I, "Ten Skills of Communication," is ten chapters, each of which focuses on one communication skill. Each chapter explains one skill, discusses why it's important, and gives you tangible instructions on how to use the skill. The "Bottom Line" sections in each chapter will summarize each skill so you can review what you've learned. These ten skills will give you the foundation you need to help you achieve success in understanding others, feeling understood yourself, and finding solutions to problems.

In Part II, "Having Difficult Conversations Skillfully," you'll find stories and scenarios that illustrate the ten communication skills in action. You'll also learn steps to boundary-setting (a very common, difficult, and important topic that I get asked about all the time) as well as tools to know when and how to end a relationship.

Throughout the book, sections titled "Practice Makes ~~Perfect~~ Easier" offer suggestions on how to practice skills and build confidence in specific aspects of communication.

By the end of this book, you will understand how to have difficult conversations: how to prepare for them, start them, and end them. You will know what to do if you're feeling blocked or when things don't go according to plan.

HOW TO USE THIS BOOK

I've jammed a lot of information in this book—many skills and a lot of lists! Read it slowly and take breaks as needed. Use it to guide and prepare you for a specific conversation you want to have or to gain new general knowledge you can refer back to when you need a refresher. You can use the Ten Skills of Communication in the order presented; they will serve as a step-by-step guide that provides structure and support to a difficult conversation. Alternatively, you can use individual skills on their own for help in certain situations. Flag your favorite sections, or take photos of them to keep in your phone so you can easily reference them when needed. There are also helpful conversation checklists in the appendices at the back of the book.

If possible, I highly recommend reading through this book with a partner, friend, family member, or anyone else who is up to learn some new skills, so that you can practice together. My partner has learned and implemented these skills along with me, which has been monumentally helpful in us both being successful communicators. As I say all the time in couples therapy, it's so great to have two people learning these skills, so that the relationship system has checkpoints: if one person doesn't catch an area to improve upon, hopefully the other person does!

IS THIS BOOK FOR *YOU*?

This book was written to help with communication in any relationship: romantic partners, friends, colleagues, bosses, employees, students, parents, children, teens . . . literally anyone you are in communication with! However, the assumption is made that you *care* about the other person in the conversation (partners, family, friends) or, at the very least, are communicating with someone with whom you need to maintain a respectful relationship (bosses, family members, teachers, students, mutual friends, coworkers, divorced co-parents). This book is for building relationships, not for debating, and not for anyone with ill intentions or a desire to manipulate others. (If that is your goal, you will soon see these steps don't apply.) If you have the desire and intention to end cycles of conflict and defensiveness, understand others, and feel more understood, then this book is for you!

After reading Part I, you'll be armed with a lot of new skills to use in conversations. After reading Part II, you'll see how to use all the skills together and how to modify them for specific scenarios. The ten skills will also help you become more aware of your own perspective as well as the perspectives of others, which will create mutual understanding. With mutual understanding, the sky's the limit when it comes to the problems you can solve and things you can achieve together. A more peaceful, structured approach to communication will leave you—and everyone you have relationships with—feeling happier and more connected.

PART I

TEN SKILLS OF COMMUNICATION

INTRODUCTION

We all communicate. And whether at work, with friends, or with family, we all want to feel understood. Through my work as a counselor, I've been able to boil down almost all miscommunications to either:

- Having your reality invalidated
- Imposing your reality onto someone else

I use the word *reality* instead of *perspective* because it encompasses so much more than just a viewpoint. The word *reality* involves an entire lived experience: how someone feels and how they think about, interpret, and understand the world around them.

We each live in in our own reality, where the things we see, feel, and think are very real and very valid. However, everyone else is also living at the same time and sometimes even in the same situation—but with their own, potentially very different, reality. To illustrate the concept of different realities, let's look at a specific example.

"THE DRESS"

In 2015, the Internet was in an uproar because of a photo of a dress. Some people saw the colors of the dress in the photo as blue and black, while others saw the colors as white and gold. (A quick web search for "the dress" will pull up an exhaustive list of photos.). On Twitter, national news channels reported that The Dress had gone viral with trending hashtags. Personal Twitter accounts defended the colors they saw and invalidated other users, describing the colors they saw and saying that everyone else who saw it differently was "wrong." Some people even tweeted how they felt left out or (hopefully jokingly) that they were ditching friends because of the difference in how they saw the colors of The Dress!

The Dress is a great parallel to what happens in communication breakdowns. There is one situation or interaction, yet two very different versions, perspectives, or *individual realities* of what is going on. One dress, yet two very different color combinations. The social media uproar around The Dress showed how far people will go to defend their own reality and claim that people who don't share their reality are wrong. People will argue and argue their own reality, because, just like with The Dress, *they literally see the situation differently than the other person,* and therefore conclude that any other perspective must be mistaken or wrong.

The parallels of The Dress to conversations can be taken even further. According to the person who took the original photo of The Dress, its actual colors were blue and black. However, even with the information about the true colors, the people who saw it as gold and white *still* viewed it as gold and white. This group didn't, or couldn't, change their view or their reality. This shows us that even with a really good argument, we often can't change how other people see a situation. Changing someone's mind is usually a futile effort!

I personally see The Dress as blue and black. It's impossible for me to see it any other way, just as the gold and white population will also not be able to change how they see it. But we can accept that we see it differently. *Accepting* that people see a different color does not mean that you *agree* and see it as that color. This key point is crucial to understanding other people and to communicating effectively—and I'll return to it again later in the book. *Accepting other realities does not mean agreeing with other realities.*

When it comes to difficult, emotionally intense conversations, one or both parties are probably in need of connection, understanding, or change in the form of solutions. Yet these needs often get buried in an argument about whose reality is "right" and whose is "wrong." Getting caught up in a fruitless debate, defending our own realities and invalidating the realities of others, distracts us from our personal conversation goals. If, instead, we can learn to accept differences in perspective (whether we agree with them or not), we can better attend to the underlying issue and work to resolve it.

The next time you have an argument or a difficult situation, ask yourself: Are you arguing about the actual underlying issue (for example, someone feeling hurt or needing a change/solution), or are you arguing that your perspective is the "right" one (for example, that you didn't mean to hurt them, there is no reason for the conversation, or that they "shouldn't feel" hurt)?

If proving one's reality takes over, the argument will go on and on, until eventually one person gets tired and reluctantly gives in or the whole topic gets swept under the rug. This leaves the underlying reason the conversation happened in the first place unresolved. Ever feel like you have the same argument repeatedly and are stuck in a cycle? This is probably why. Realities were defended, and that left no room for realities to be understood (by validating or describing—see Chapters 6 and 7), and so you never got to the point of finding solutions (see Chapter 8). No solution means the problem will keep resurfacing.

If you can accept, and then validate, someone else's reality, then you can understand them, and then they really *feel* understood. When they feel understood, they calm down. They stop defending their reality because you have shown them that you understand. By validating someone, you are modeling the behavior you want to see, forming a connection, and putting them at ease. They can now be open to hear *your* reality, and, as a result, you'll both be able to focus on collaborating to find solutions.

If we feel as though no one understands us, we can feel alone, angry, and depressed. When we don't understand someone else, they can also feel alone, angry, and depressed. Other reactions can include becoming frustrated, defensive, or argumentative. Miscommunication and lack of understanding create cycles of distress. If instead we can communicate effectively, so that both parties feel heard and understood, we can avoid defensiveness and negative feelings and move forward in peace, working as a team to find solutions to the problems we face. And that is what this entire book will help you learn to do!

HOW COGNITIVE BEHAVIOR THERAPY (CBT) HELPS COMMUNICATION

Cognitive Behavior Therapy (CBT)[3] is an evidence-based psychotherapy model that helps people connect situations, thoughts, and reactions. I often use CBT with clients in our first few sessions because it is a powerful foundation for understanding ourselves and why we react to things the way we do. Knowing the concepts of the CBT "cognitive model" will be useful in applying skills of communication and managing any blocks that may come up.

To illustrate the cognitive model, imagine a situation you have recently experienced in which you were either curious about your reaction ("Why did I get so pissed off about that?") or would like to react differently in the future ("I'd love to not raise my voice so much!").

Now ask yourself:

- What was the situation?
- What was your reaction? Break this reaction down into three categories:
    - emotional (what did you feel?)
    - behavioral (what did you do?)
    - physical (what did you feel in your body?)

We'll circle back to your personal example, but first I'll illustrate the cognitive model with a hypothetical example:

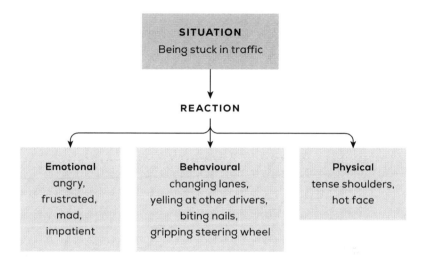

Most often, we use language such as, "I was angry because I was stuck in traffic." A statement like this implies that *the situation was the cause of the reaction.*

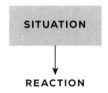

However, if the situation is the cause of the reaction, then any time someone is in traffic, the same reaction would occur.

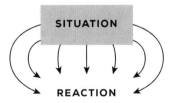

Yet we know this is not the case. People have very different reactions to being stuck in traffic.

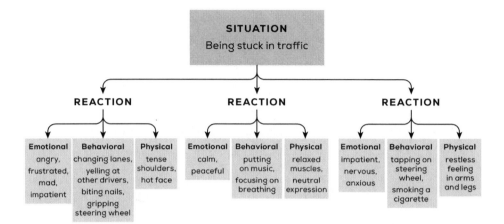

Therefore, there must be a missing variable causing or supporting the angry reaction. What might that be?

It's our thoughts!

The concept to take away from the cognitive model is that *we are reacting to our thoughts about the situation, not to the situation itself.*

Below is an example of the same situation causing two very different reactions because of different thoughts.

This example illustrates that it's not the situation that causes the reaction, it's *the thoughts about the situation that cause the reaction.* In order to change our reaction, we need to do something about our thoughts!

Now, I'm not telling you to change your thoughts. In fact, in CBT, those thoughts are called "Automatic Thoughts" because you can't control when they come up or what their content is; they're unconscious and immediate brain activity—your brain trying to make sense of the world given your past experiences and beliefs.

Ever try to change your thoughts? Let's try now. Don't think of an umbrella. Whatever you do, don't picture one in your mind. Don't make it a pink umbrella. It's impossible! Now try to think only of umbrellas for a full

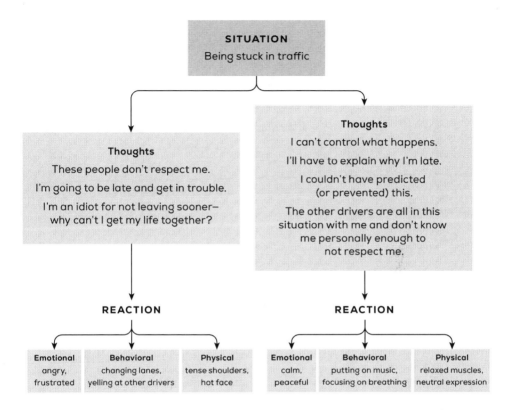

minute—don't think about anything else. Also impossible! It can be frustrating that it's your brain, yet you feel such little control over what it does and does not do. This is especially true when you are having reactions you want to change. If your reaction is to your thoughts, yet you can't choose or control what thoughts you have, what do you do!?

First, you can bring awareness, or mindfulness, to your Automatic Thoughts. Most of the time, we aren't aware of what we're thinking, which is great because it's highly efficient. If I had to consciously think of moving every finger on my keyboard as I was writing this sentence, for example, "Okay, I am going to press the K key now"—it would take me forever! However, when you have a reaction (emotional, physical, or behavioral) that you want to change, that is your signal to bring some form of awareness, or mindfulness, to your thoughts.

To help identify Automatic Thoughts, ask yourself:

- "What's going through my mind?"
- "What am I imagining or predicting might happen?"
- "Do I imagine a worst-case scenario?"
- "How am I feeling about myself?"
- "Am I remembering a past similar situation?"

Now you've brought some awareness to your thoughts. However, since you can't *change* your thoughts, what is the next thing to do with those thoughts?

Challenge them.

Our default mode is not only to be unaware of most of our thoughts (as stated before), but also to believe that our thoughts are *100 percent true.* Again, this belief in our thoughts can be efficient, but it can also get us into trouble. In the traffic example, the person was thinking, "These people don't respect me." But is that true? How does the person know? What evidence do they have that their thought is true? Untrue? On a percentage scale of 1 to 100, how true would you say the thought is? Another thought the person stuck in traffic had was, "I'm going to be late and get into trouble." This might seem very true, as the brain is taking past experiences (where they've been late and gotten into trouble) and applying that information to predict the future. In that case, we can say that they will most likely be in trouble, so then they can ask, "How can I cope with that?"

Learning how to challenge thoughts for accuracy or truthfulness, and gaining confidence in your ability to cope with the predictions your brain is giving you, can be very helpful for reacting differently to situations.

CBT skills, specifically the cognitive model, can help with conversations by increasing self-awareness. Through identifying Automatic Thoughts, we can understand *why* we've got an urge to react, behave, or feel a certain way. Knowing why we do the things we do can help change reactions to make them more productive. CBT also helps in that it causes us to be more aware of what might be going on in other people's minds and why they

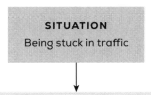

SITUATION
Being stuck in traffic

AT: These people don't respect me.

Challenge the thought: Mostly untrue. 2% true.

Replace with an adaptive (or more realistic) thought: These people are stuck in traffic just like me; they don't know me personally but are just trying to get ahead of everyone.

AT: I'm going to get in trouble.

Challenge the thought: Probably true. 98% true (I've gotten in trouble the last 3 times I was late, but maybe the boss isn't in today or is also late).

Cope: I might get in trouble at work; if that's the case, I'll use my skills from this book to have a conversation and describe my perspective, and come up with a solution that helps the situation.

might be reacting the way they are in a given situation. This can help us understand others' perspectives and leads to a more productive conversation because *they* feel better understood. Awareness of self and others are such important skills, and therefore you will see prompts to identify Automatic Thoughts in many future sections of this book.

There is a lot more to CBT that I won't go into in this book, but three main takeaways to help troubleshoot emotional regulation are:

1. Become aware of your thoughts.
2. Remember that just because you're having a thought doesn't mean it's true, or 100 percent true. Challenge the truth of the thought, then replace it with a thought that is more true.
3. Think about how to cope with the potential worst-case situation (this may require some skills and help from a therapist).

If you want to explore further, I encourage you to find a CBT therapist to connect with. See the Recommended Resources in the back of the book (page 273) for suggestions on where to find one.

PRACTICE MAKES ~~PERFECT~~ EASIER

Remember at the beginning of this section you were asked to come up with an example of a recent situation in which you were curious about your reaction or wanted to change your reaction? Use a blank cognitive model to help draw this out. (See Appendix I, page 261, for a blank cognitive model worksheet.) What was the situation? What was the reaction? What were your automatic thoughts? Did your thoughts turn out to be true? How true were your thoughts on a scale of 0 to 100? Have you ever been in a similar (or even the same) situation but reacted differently? How were your thoughts different? Does knowing what you were thinking help the reaction make more sense?

Being aware of thoughts in the moment takes time. You probably won't be able to remember this new skill in the moment for a while, and that's okay! Do it as soon after the situation as you can. Keep practicing, and it will become easier and easier—and it will be worth it!

Another tip is that when identifying Automatic Thoughts, it can be helpful to watch them as nonjudgmentally as possible. I often see clients become frustrated, shameful, guilty, or angry at the fact they're even having a thought! As illustrated before with the umbrella exercise, we can't control our thoughts. It can be helpful to think of them like clouds passing in the sky; to attach meaning to them or try to exert control over them will not get you very far. In fact, trying to push away thoughts usually makes them push back even harder! Instead, try your best to bring non-judgmental curiosity to your Automatic Thoughts: "Oh, that's interesting that popped into my mind first; I wonder why that is. . . ." or "Wow, that really untrue thought was my first reaction . . . let me see if I can think of something that is more realistic, rational, and true." Remind yourself that your thoughts aren't your "fault" and don't mean anything about you as a person. Being gentle with yourself will make the process of being mindful a lot more comfortable and productive!

BOTTOM LINE

Now that you've learned a bit about different realities (as illustrated by The Dress) and used the CBT cognitive model to explore reactions and why they occur, you're ready to move on the Ten Skills of Communication. Keep The Dress and the cognitive model in mind as you read about and learn how to skillfully have difficult conversations.

Chapter 1

SET PERSONAL GOALS

10 SKILLS OF COMMUNICATION

1. Set Personal Goals
2. Choose a Time, Place, and Platform
3. Calm Down (Enough)
4. Remember to Listen
5. State Common Goals
6. Validate
7. Describe
8. Find Solutions
9. Offer Positive Reinforcement
10. Practice Self-Care

INTRODUCTION

Welcome to the Ten Skills of Communication! The first four skills presented are for you to use *before* a conversation. You may be wanting to cut right to the action—the conversation itself—but in the next four chapters, I will make a case for why preparing for conversations is extremely helpful in achieving success, and how to apply these skills in spontaneous conversations when there isn't designated time to prepare.

Communication has a purpose, but sometimes it's easy to lose sight of what that purpose is. This first chapter discusses the importance of setting personal communication goals before having a conversation. If you can *be-*

come aware of the intention of your communication, you can check that it's realistic, fair, and achievable. Achievable goals set the foundation for effective, successful communication.

SETTING PERSONAL GOALS: WHY IT'S IMPORTANT

Have you ever had an argument that morphs into other arguments? Or left a conversation thinking, "What the @$*! just happened?"

During emotionally charged conversations, it can be tough to stick to the point. If you know you're going into a potentially intense conversation, clarifying (with yourself) your goals for the conversation *before* it happens can help you not get derailed or sidetracked.

Setting goals is not only helpful for focusing a conversation, but it can also do something else even more important: help you know whether a conversation will be productive and worth having. For example, have you ever tried to change someone's mind? It's very nearly impossible! Have you ever tried to convince someone not to feel an emotion they're feeling? This is also rarely possible! Remember The Dress? We can't make someone see colors they don't see. By setting goals, you can determine the possible outcome of a conversation before it even happens. You can know if you will be successful or unsuccessful depending on how realistic your personal goals are.

Another reason that specific personal goals are helpful to you is that you can reflect back on a conversation after it's completed and check in on if you achieved your goals. Sometimes we get lost and don't really know if a conversation was productive. If you have goals laid out beforehand, you'll know if you need to approach the topic again or if it has been resolved.

SETTING PERSONAL GOALS: HOW TO DO IT

To set specific goals for a conversation, start by asking yourself:

- What do I want to get out of this conversation?
- What is the problem or issue I am having right now?

* Why is this conversation necessary?
* What am I hoping to achieve? What do I want? What is my ideal outcome?

Now ask,

* Is this goal realistic, fair, and achievable?

Realistic, fair, and achievable goals for communication fall into two categories:

1. *To understand* the other person:

* To get to know their perspective through curiosity
* To show them you understand through reflection and validation

2. *To describe* your situation, possibly with:

* Intent to be understood
* Intent to motivate
* Intent to express emotion
* Intent to create emotion in someone else

Notice that the goal of describing includes *intentions* and not *expectations*. You can be aware that your goal of describing has a potential desired outcome, but you must also be aware that you cannot control whether that outcome happens. Your reality and perspective are valid, and it's very fair to want to be understood, yet we can't force people to agree with us or even to understand us.

Motivating someone to change is precisely that: *giving them motivation*. Motivation can come in the form of describing your reality, or coming up with compromises and solutions to try. These techniques can help motivate someone to action but cannot *guarantee* action.

Examples of Describing Your Reality

Intent to be understood	Telling someone about a hard day at work
	Telling someone how their comment hurt you
Intent to motivate	Explaining your boundaries to someone with the intent that they will respect them
	Talking about a chores list with your kids or partner with the intent that they will be more active in doing those chores
Intent to express emotion	Singing a song, journaling, or creating a piece of art
Intent to create emotion in someone else	Giving someone a compliment
	Saying something mean

Techniques to achieve the goals of understanding and describing are presented in detail later in the book—see Chapter 6 ("Validate") and Chapter 7 ("Describe"). For now, having goals you can be successful with is the first step.

Let's look at some examples of unrealistic, unfair, or unachievable personal goals versus realistic, fair, and achievable alternatives.

Unrealistic, Unachievable, or Unfair Goals	Realistic, Achievable, and Fair Goals
To change the other person's mind	To understand their process (understand)
	To describe my point of view (describe with intent to be understood)
To get them to agree with me	To communicate my boundaries respectfully (describe with intent to motivate)
To prove or convince them they're wrong	To describe my perspective (describe with intent to be understood)
	To understand why they reacted/felt/said/thought certain ways and things (understand)

Unrealistic, Unachievable, or Unfair Goals	Realistic, Achievable, and Fair Goals
To convince them to feel a certain way	To understand why they're feeling a certain way (understand)
To convince them not to feel a certain way	To come up with solutions for future similar situations (to understand or describe with intent to motivate)
	To describe that it was not my intention to cause them to feel/not feel that way (describe with intent to be understood)
To get them to do what I want them to do	To express how their actions are making me feel (describe with intent to motivate)
	To communicate boundaries (describe with intent to motivate)
	To come up with solutions to try so this situation doesn't happen again (describe with intent to motivate)
To make them understand me	To describe my reality (describe with intent to be understood)

Goal-Setting Examples

Below are some specific scenarios of goal-setting, including what's realistic and what's unrealistic.

1. Convincing someone not to feel a certain way

You're having an argument with your partner. They took something you said out of context, and they are feeling hurt.

Unrealistic goal: Convince them not to feel hurt (because that's not what you meant to do!).

Realistic goal: Listen to why they're feeling that way (understand), describe how that was not your intention (describe with intent to be understood), and come up with solutions for future similar situations (describe with intent to motivate).

This example underscores the difference between what we can and can't control. We can't control someone else's mind, how they think, or what they feel (if we could, I'd be out of a job!). So, instead, conversational effort goes into what you can control, such as understanding the other person and having them feel understood, describing your own perspective, and coming up with solutions.

2. "Whose turn is it to do the dishes?"

This is a very, very, *very* common issue among cohabitants. You come home to see a sink full of dirty dishes. You were the one who did them last, so you're pissed that your roommate hasn't cleaned them. Something needs to change!

> Unrealistic goal: Get them to do the dishes.
>
> Realistic goal: Express the disrespect and frustration you feel when they don't do the dishes (describe with intent to be understood). Find new solutions or compromises to try (describe with intent to motivate).

In this example, the unrealistic goal is to change the behavior. The realistic goal is to let your roommate in on how you are feeling about their mess. The underlying *theme of feeling disrespected* will help focus the conversation on solving that, rather than trying to solve how the dishes "should" be done.

3. When they're just plain "wrong"

This is clearly a hypothetical example, but it can be applied to many scenarios and illustrates what realistic goals are when you have two very different realities. Imagine your friend thinks 2 + 2 = 5. What would a conversation around this look like? What might your goals be?

Unrealistic goal: "Prove" to them that 2 + 2 = 4 because they are wrong!

Realistic goal: Understand their reasoning behind why they think that (understand). Describe that you think 2 + 2 = 4 and why (present evidence and describ with intent to motivate).

In this example, it's important to note that you might be looking for a debate instead of a resolution. In debating, a different set of communication tactics apply. The communication skills in this book are for developing relationships with people where you have a stake in a productive, peaceful outcome. If you want to have a conversation about this with a realistic goal, choosing a goal of understanding the other person's reasoning and describing your own reasoning is the way to go.

PRACTICE MAKES PERFECT EASIER

Think about a conversation you've had in the past or one you are hoping to have in the future. Write down your goals. Then review what kind of words you chose. Unrealistic goals tend to include language like "change," "make them," "prove," and "convince." Realistic goals, in contrast, contain words like "describe" and "understand."

"What If My Personal Goals Don't Include 'Understand' or 'Describe'?"

If your goals don't include describing or understanding, have a good think about what you're trying to achieve with the conversation. If you are trying to get someone to do something or to change them, well, you can certainly try! This will be tough and could even be damaging to your relationship. Personal goal-setting is about understanding the freedom that others have, accepting the things we can't control, and then setting goals we *can* achieve.

Too Many Goals, Too Little Time

After you've taken the time to think about and note down your goals for a conversation, count them. Remind yourself that, while your reality makes sense to you, this might be completely new information to the other person. Bringing up too many points waters everything down, making it difficult for the other person to fully take in the information, understand it, process its importance, and come up with solutions as needed. Three goals are the maximum I'd recommend, but one or two goals is ideal. If you've come up with a list of more than three goals, you can either:

1. Find an underlying theme that will now be the singular, unifying goal that you wish to communicate; or
2. Split the goals into separate conversations.

If you choose option 1 (finding an underlying theme), you can ask yourself:

- What do these goals all have in common?
- How do I feel about each of these goals?
- What do these goals say about our relationship in general?
- What do these goals say about how I feel I'm being treated?
- What am I hoping the outcome of all these goals will be?

After asking these questions, you may find that there are similar feelings, themes of treatment, or outcome goals that come up. These themes are now the main goal to address, rather than the specific situations.

If you choose option 2 (splitting the goals into separate conversations), write out your goals and prioritize them. Which needs the most attention?

If they are all tied for the top spot, is there one goal for which the conversation will be easiest? Choose that one; it will help set the stage and build your confidence for success with future, more complex topics and conversations.

Here's an example in which you can choose between finding an underlying theme and splitting your goals into separate conversations. During a conversation with your partner about them being late, you also feel the urge to bring up the time you felt they were overly flirtatious with a waiter.

Unproductive option: Change topics and bring up the flirting.

Productive option 1: Save the flirting for a different conversation. Make a mental note or a note in your phone.

Productive option 2: Think about the underlying, unifying theme of both topics that came up. For example, both being late and being flirtatious with a stranger left you feeling disrespected and not good enough. Your new, singular goal could be describing your feelings (and you could add solution finding, covered in Chapter 8, to help you feel better as well!).

Setting Goals in Spontaneous Conversations

Sometimes goal-setting beforehand is impossible; some conversations happen spontaneously. If you find yourself in a spontaneous conversation, think to yourself, "What seems to be the purpose of this conversation?" To answer this requires awareness in the moment, which is a skill that takes time and practice to develop but gets easier the more you do it! Once you have the answer to this question, you can help focus on the goal(s) and steer the conversation where it needs to go. Is someone in need of being understood? Do solutions need to be found?

What to Do If Someone Brings Up Their Own Goals

If other things come up in conversation besides the things you want to discuss (perhaps the other person is bringing up their own goals), awareness is key. Remind yourself of your goals, and be aware of the goals the other person has brought up. Make a mental note (or a physical note) to save the least pertinent goals for a separate conversation. You might even discuss this with the other person and set a later time for that conversation. This way, the conversation you are presently having will have a clear ending, instead of being derailed by multiple issues, and it's more likely that you'll achieve your goals. I'll discuss different specific types of conversation derailing, such as victim mentality, defensiveness, interrupting, and more, later in the book.

Stuck in a Cycle: Getting Derailed and Having Incomplete Conversations

Sometimes we get caught in a repeating cycle of unproductive conversations with another person and end up getting so derailed that we get exhausted and end the conversation without any resolution or achievement of goals. In cases like this, clarity is extremely helpful. Next time you are preparing for a conversation with a person with whom you've experienced this repeating cycle, write out your personal goals, and then share them with the other person at the beginning of the conversation. Better yet, give them your list beforehand so they can think about their own reality and possible solutions if needed. If both of you are prepared for a specific outcome, it will help keep the conversation focused—now you'll have two people keeping things on track. This should get easier with practice! If the conversation is spontaneous or started by the other person, bring in your awareness and pause the conversation to go over goals together. What needs to be addressed now, and what should be saved for a separate conversation? If you are both on board with practicing this, one of you will be able to remember this important step to help stay on track.

What to Do If Someone's Personal Goal Is Unclear

If you are in a spontaneous conversation that someone else has initiated, and you have done your best to guess their goal(s) but are still unsure, you can ask them something like:

* "I'd love to help you out with what you need from this conversation, but I'm a little unclear on what that is. Could you help me by telling me what you need?"

or

* "I'm curious what you're hoping to get out of this conversation. Could you help me understand so we can make the most of it?"

If their answer is unclear, you can usually safely assume their goal is to have their reality validated and to be listened to (describe with intent to be understood). (More about how to validate is explained in Chapter 6.)

PRACTICE MAKES ~~PERFECT~~ EASIER

To practice identifying goals in spontaneous conversations, ask yourself, "What do I think the purpose of this conversation is?" as it applies to any casual conversation you have during the day. Bringing this awareness of the purpose of any communication to your daily interactions will greatly help you to know the difference between goals that are achievable and goals that are not. Once you have practiced this skill so often that it becomes second nature, it will be immediately accessible during more intense spontaneous conversations.

Here are some examples of goals within everyday conversations:

1. In your conversation with your barista, *their* goal is to know your coffee order (understand), *your* goal is to communicate what you'd like (describe), and, hopefully, that description will get them to make your coffee order as you prefer (intent to motivate).
2. With your colleague, your goal is to find out when a deadline is scheduled (understand).
3. When comforting a friend who has gone through a breakup, your goal is to listen and validate their feelings (understand).

4. With your partner, your goal is to hear how they're feeling by asking about their day (understand), then to express how you're feeling about your day (describe), and maybe plan for dinner (describe with intent to motivate).

BOTTOM LINE

Setting personal goals is an essential first step to any successful conversation, as clear goals help with sticking to the point and determining if the conversation will be productive. Realistic, fair, and achievable goals will fall into the categories of "understand" or "describe" (with intent to be understood and/or motivate). Knowing what your goals are will also allow you to recognize when the communication has been successfully completed.

Chapter 2

CHOOSE A TIME,
PLACE, AND PLATFORM

10 SKILLS OF COMMUNICATION

1. Set Personal Goals
2. **Choose a Time, Place, and Platform**
3. Calm Down (Enough)
4. Remember to Listen
5. State Common Goals
6. Validate
7. Describe
8. Find Solutions
9. Offer Positive Reinforcement
10. Practice Self-Care

INTRODUCTION

Ever had a day (or week or month) that feels like it's just one stressful thing after another? And that you just don't have the capacity for anything more? Things like fatigue, having had a stressful day at work, or conducting a conversation over text messaging can make a huge difference in our reactions; therefore, the setting and timing you choose for a conversation can affect its outcome. In Dialectical Behavior Therapy (DBT), these are called "vulnerability factors."[4] They are environments, events, moods, physical states, or substances that get in the way of our ability to emotionally regulate. Vulnerability factors cause us to become more at risk of getting swept away by emotions. (In the next chapter, I'll talk more about the importance of staying calm during a conversation and tools to achieve that.) In this chapter, I'll explain how choosing an appropriate time, place, and platform for a conversation can help reduce vulnerability factors and lead to the most successful outcome possible.

CHOOSING A TIME: WHY IT'S IMPORTANT

Choosing a time for a conversation is all about how to set yourself, and the other person, up for success. If you are extremely tired, how well do you think the conversation will go? If the other person is experiencing other vulnerability factors, such as having had a stressful day at work or several drinks with a friend, how might that change the outcome? Finding the optimal time for a conversation will help you feel safe, comfortable, and able to achieve your communication goals.

CHOOSING A TIME: HOW TO DO IT

Just as we did in Chapter 1 when we discussed setting personal goals, let's look at what we can and can't control in a situation. While some constraints in a situation may be out of our control, others we can at least work around. These can be things such as fatigue, diet (type or amount of food), a prior distressing event, hormonal changes, substance use, life stress, and more.

Sometimes we have the urge to speak about things in "the heat of the moment." The appeal of this is obvious: we want to address the situation right then and there, so that its importance is evident to the other person and the issues don't linger. Although the urge for immediacy is a valid one, I suggest you not have "in-the-moment" conversations if at all possible. When you've seen specific behaviors, boundary crosses, or arguments that happen again and again, or if you've witnessed something for the first time that you want to address, having conversations "out of the moment" sets you up for more success because you've had time to think, calm down, and prepare for the conversation. *Out-of-the-moment conversations can help set you up for successful in-the-moment conversations in the future,* as both people will be on the same page with what to expect and how to handle the situation immediately when it might arise later. For example, "Remember what we spoke about when it comes to misinterpretations of jokes you make?" (More on setting this up in the chapters on solution finding and boundary-setting.)

When thinking about choosing the best time for a conversation, try asking yourself the following questions:

1. When are my four basic needs of safety, food, water, and sleep most satiated? We all know how much these things can affect our ability to emotionally regulate, stay calm, and stick to the point.
2. When are the other person's four basic needs of safety, food, water, and sleep most satiated?
3. Are there patterns of unsuccessful conversations with this person? If so, what time of day or month or year did they take place?
4. How urgent is this conversation? Sometimes we need to have a conversation as quickly as possible. This is where your best judgment will balance the immediacy of the conversation versus the potential times that could lead to the most success.
5. Are other things taking up a lot of my/their attention? My/their mental or emotional energy? Things such as work or school deadlines, schedule changes, stress in other relationships, trips together, time apart, illness, injury, or big events can be reasons to put a conversation on hold until you are both able to give it your full attention.

Again, use your best judgment as to how these factors may affect you *both*. It can be easy to know how you feel, but taking a moment to put yourself in the other person's shoes can help you know if it's really the right time for a conversation. If you're unsure of when to have a conversation, I suggest erring on the side of compromise in favor of the other person. Why? Because you will most likely have had more time to prepare, since you are the one raising the issue.

Preparing Others for Conversation (aka "We Need to Talk")

"We need to talk." These four words typically mean you're going to have a conversation that leaves you gutted—maybe for reasons you're unsure of, but which you get to guess and stress about until the conversation happens. There are pros and cons to the "we need to talk" tactic of trying to prepare someone for a difficult conversation. There are situations where it's not appropriate, and there are situations where it's helpful—and there are ways to do it as gently as possible. Let's first look at the pros and cons of giving warning that a difficult conversation is imminent:

Pros:

- It gives the other person time to prepare mentally and emotionally.
- It's respectful of a busy schedule.
- It could be a relief for the other person to know that a resolution is on the way!

Cons:

- It potentially stresses out the other person—their Automatic Thoughts run wild!
- The other person might come into the conversation in a distressed state or in a defensive mode.

When to use the "we need to talk" tactic

- If the other person is not much of a worrier
- If they probably have a sense of what is going on already
- If they generally don't like surprises

When not to use the "we need to talk" tactic

- If they're already a very anxious or worried person (a warning could cause distress)
- If you know the individual hasn't responded well to this approach in the past
- If an issue is coming out of the blue or is immediate (giving a warning will just make the other person wonder what is going on)
- If they might avoid the conversation, whether intentionally or accidentally

If you have decided that giving a heads-up is your best option, there is an easy way to gently cue another person that you want to have a conversation, and to give a warning that's not ominous and doesn't lead to them stressing over what the content of the conversation will be. To do this, simply let them in on more information! Be specific about your goals for the conversation.

Example A: "Hey, can we please talk about the chore list before we go to bed?"

In this example, there is a specific topic: the chores. Now the other person knows what the talk will be about and doesn't need to worry about the content of the conversation (such as, "They said we need to talk tonight. Are they going to break up with me?").

Example B: "When you get home, I'd like to talk about the chores list. Is that okay?"

This example is specific and gets the other person's buy-in for having the conversation. You are seeing if they are available to talk and then asking if your proposed time will work for them. This shows your care and respect for their mental and emotional capacity to have a discussion. If they are not available, ask them to suggest another *specific time* that will work.

CHOOSING A PLACE AND PLATFORM: WHY IT'S IMPORTANT

Place is the physical location, and platform is the medium through which you have the conversation (for example, direct message, video chat, or in person). In this day and age, there are so many great ways to connect with others, each with their own specific strengths and drawbacks. Ever had a miscommunication due to a misunderstanding of tone in a text or email? Ever gotten so flustered in a face-to-face conversation you'd wished you had time to collect your thoughts? Choosing the right place and platform can set you up for success and safety, and mitigate misunderstanding.

CHOOSING A PLACE AND PLATFORM: HOW TO DO IT

Consider the goals for a conversation you want to have and the time you've chosen for it. Then look at the table that follows to see how the pros and cons might fit into your specific situation.

PROS AND CONS OF DIFFERENT MEDIA		
Media	**Pros**	**Cons**
Face-to-Face/Video	• Nonverbal cues, such as tone, facial expressions, and body language convey a lot of information, especially if you are unsure of how someone might react. • It's harder for the other person to ignore/avoid you. • It shows you've taken the time and made the effort to see them in person.	• It can be challenging to take time and space to gather thoughts, if needed. • It can be easier to get derailed by emotions, which can lead to saying/doing things you don't mean. • Depending on the video, you might not be able to see all body language.
Phone/Voice-Only	• You get to hear tone. • You get to roll your eyes without being seen! • You can have notes with goals or things you want to say/avoid saying.	• It can be challenging to take time and space to gather thoughts, if needed. • You miss important facial expressions and body language. • Either party can hang up at any moment and shut down the conversation prematurely, or avoid the conversation when it gets difficult.
Written/Text	• It gives time for both parties to think and respond/react. • It helps you stick to your conversation goals because you can refer back to them more easily throughout the interaction. • If you are a strong writer, it can be a good way to communicate. • It limits the possibility of interruption. • It's a good option if your two individual "ideal times" don't align.	• You might not know if/when the other person received or read your message. • You might not know if your message is being delivered at a good time for the other person. • Lack of nonverbal cues (such as tone) can lead to miscommunication. • It might seem that you don't consider the issue/person important. • There might not be confidentiality; the other person might share your messages with others.

What points are most relevant to the conversation you want to have? If you know someone well enough to assume how they might react, nonverbal cues may not be so important. If nonverbal cues *are* important, it's best to have the conversation in person or over video chat. If it's important to allow the other person (or yourself) sufficient time to process and respond, then a written platform, such as email or text, might be a better option. Text can also be a great option with people you know well who can easily guess your tone.

If you think an in-person platform might work for your conversation, another question to ask yourself is, "Is there a need for privacy, and/or do we need others present?" This is especially important when dealing with sensitive or highly personal issues.

It can be tough to know where to have a conversation that will help set it up for success. Below are some questions to consider when choosing the place and platform for your conversation, in order to achieve the most successful outcome.

- Are there any safety issues (emotional or physical)?
- What has been successful in the past with this specific person or in a similar situation with someone else?
- What has not been successful in the past?
- Would the situation benefit from mediation from a family or couples therapist, an HR representative, or another third party being present?
- Do you need professional input (a human resources representative, a lawyer, etc.)?
- Do we need someone to be taking notes and documenting the situation?
- Could the other person feel guilty, embarrassed, or ashamed if others are present?

Going for a walk together can be a great solution. Depending on the place you choose for the walk, it can be very private or not as private, but, in general, other people won't be able to listen in because you're on the move. You also can pick up on nonverbal cues but aren't forced to look directly at each other the entire time.

Where Not to Have Conversations

One thing I strongly suggest is that you don't have conversations while lying in bed. (People with sleep issues, this especially applies to you!). A bed is a place for being calm, asleep, or intimate. It is not a place for stimulating, emotionally intense conversations. If someone is in bed, they are hopefully either just waking up or just going to sleep; neither is a good time for emotional conversations, which require focus.

Time, Place, and Platform for Spontaneous Conversations

Sometimes conversations can come up organically, at a time and place we didn't intend. Maybe the other person has brought up the issue. If this is the case, use the techniques for setting personal goals laid out in the previous chapter to roll with the goal at hand. Alternatively, use boundary-setting techniques (Chapter 14) to ask for more time to prepare for the conversation.

PRACTICE MAKES ~~PERFECT~~ EASIER

Think about some past difficult or intense conversations you've had. When and where did they take place? How did they turn out? Do you think the times, places, and/or platform affected the outcomes? Are there alternative times, places, or platforms that might have led to different (better or worse) outcomes?

Learning to assess past experiences to see what was successful or what could be done differently is a great skill to develop for future conversations.

BOTTOM LINE

The timing of a conversation, as well as the place and platform, can greatly impact your chances of a successful interaction. By thinking ahead and doing some deliberate planning, you can reduce the vulnerability factors for both people, and set yourself up for success.

Chapter 3

CALM DOWN (ENOUGH)

10 SKILLS OF COMMUNICATION

1. Set Personal Goals
2. Choose a Time, Place, and Platform
3. **Calm Down (Enough)**
4. Remember to Listen
5. State Common Goals
6. Validate
7. Describe
8. Find Solutions
9. Offer Positive Reinforcement
10. Practice Self-Care

INTRODUCTION

Do you hate being told to calm down? Most of us do (myself included!). Though it's true that this can be extremely aggravating, being calm is essential to having productive conversations. We've all been there: emotions take over, and we do or say something in the heat of the moment that we later regret. Even in counselor training, we learn that the bare minimum for counseling (or even a productive conversation) to take place is *two people, one of whom is calm.* Therefore, before attempting to communicate, remind yourself that you must be calm enough to have a conversation stay on track.

Now that you've learned about setting personal goals and choosing a time, place, and platform, I'll explain how to get calm before, and even stay calm during, conversations.

CALMING DOWN (ENOUGH): WHY IT'S IMPORTANT

For a conversation not get to derailed by intense emotion, we must do our best to regulate ourselves before and during the conversation. Regulating emotions does not mean being devoid of them; rather, calming down is about being able to manage your emotions so that you're *calm enough* to have a *successful conversation*.

If you know the conversation might increase your emotions, that's okay! It's great to have that foresight, and it's completely valid to have emotions. Knowing that emotional escalation might happen, calming down helps you enter the conversation at a lower baseline. It's like entering the dialogue at a 2/10 intensity rather than a 6/10 intensity. If you enter at a 2, you have a lot more room to work with before things get too intense to continue!

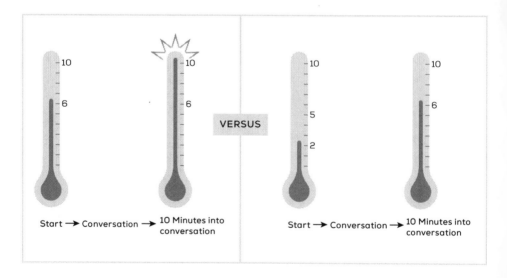

CALMING DOWN (ENOUGH): HOW TO DO IT

A plethora of relaxation, grounding, and breathing exercises are available on the Internet. I like to give my clients a wide array of techniques, so they can choose the ones that fit for them. Not every technique will be useful for everyone; techniques are a very personal thing. If you already have some that work for you and can remain calm during emotionally charged conversations, feel free to skip ahead to the next chapter. Otherwise, read on!

Calming Down before Conversations

Calming down prior to a conversation helps create the lowest possible baseline of emotional arousal. If you have the luxury of preparing for a conversation, practice your favorite calming techniques or choose from the following suggestions. I have broken down the "before conversations" calming techniques into four categories: breathing techniques, grounding techniques, logistical preparation, and emotional preparation. These four categories will cover physical, practical, and emotional preparations you can undertake to achieve a calmer state. You can also practice these techniques daily so you're a calmer and more grounded person overall, which can be beneficial when spontaneous conversations arise!

Breathing Techniques

Sometimes clients say, "Breathing exercises don't work for me." To which I reply, "What are they supposed to do that they're not doing?" A lot of the time, the client realizes that they aren't sure, or that their expectation is that breathing will remove anxious thoughts. Explaining *why* we use breathing can clear up the confusion.

When someone is panicked, how are they breathing? With short, fast, shallow breaths (think of anyone you've seen in a horror movie). What happens to their heart rate? It speeds up. These physical symptoms are part of a reaction we have, sometimes called the fight/flight response. This response kicks in when we feel threatened. In fact, it's a great system, because the fast-paced breathing jams oxygen into our bodies at a high rate, and our fast heart rate pumps the oxygenated blood into our muscles so we can efficiently fight or flee (that is, run away!). Unfortunately, our brain is not good at realizing the difference between a physical threat versus an emotional threat; it just interprets "threat" and can go into the fight/flight mode before or during an intense conversation.

So, what can we do to help calm this fight/flight system? Most of us can't directly control our heart rates (unless you're a professional magician or free diver), and we can't control most of the other systems affected by the fight/flight mode either (such as hormonal changes or sweating). We *can,* however, control our breathing.

Slowing down our breathing helps the body return to a calm state. We are able to access the parts of the brain linked to problem-solving, logic, and all that other good stuff, rather than reacting in the instinctual, threat-management part of the brain that is active during the fight/flight response. Focusing on breathing might not *remove* anxious thoughts, but it can help give your brain a task to focus on that will distract you from the thoughts while also calming you down.

There are a lot of breathing exercises out there. Here are my two favorites:

Paced Breathing:[5] The point of paced breathing is to breathe out for longer than you breathe in. It's the opposite of those short, shallow, inhale-focused fight/flight breaths. Some people like a ratio of 7 counts to 11 counts (called "7:11 breathing"). I personally like 4:6 breathing. Do whatever works for you!

> **Practice Makes ~~Perfect~~ Easier:** Breathe in for 1, 2, 3, 4, pause, then breathe out for 1, 2, 3, 4, 5, 6, pause. Repeat for 3 to 5 breaths.

Box Breathing: Box breathing helps us achieve slow, consistent breaths. In this exercise, there are points where you hold the inhale or exhale, which can be extremely helpful for those who tend to breathe too quickly or hyperventilate.

Practice Makes ~~Perfect~~ Easier: Breathe in for 4, hold for 4, out for 4, hold for 4. Repeat for 3 to 5 breaths.

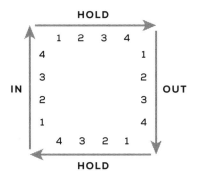

Grounding Techniques

Sometimes when emotions get heightened, we can feel swept away. We start thinking about the past or future, or we feel disconnected from our bodies. To counteract that process, here is my favorite grounding technique.

Five Senses: Look around the room and notice five things you see, four things you hear, three things you can touch or feel, two things you can smell, and one thing you can taste.

The numbers don't matter, as it's more about tuning in to your senses. Here's why using the five senses is helpful:

1. It grounds you in your present time and place;
2. It grounds you in your body; and
3. It distracts your mind from anxious thoughts.

These effects can be extremely helpful if you feel overwhelmed by uncomfortable emotions or distressing thoughts about the past or future.

There are a lot of other grounding techniques on the Internet; if you work with a therapist, they can recommend others too. Explore some more, and give them a try!

Logistical Preparation

Feeling prepared for a conversation can also aid in feeling calm. You can prepare by going over the communication skills in this book and thinking about specific examples of what you might say. Remind yourself of the skills, strengths, and resources available to cope with difficult situations. You can also ask yourself which Automatic Thoughts might come up during the conversation? Are they true? Talk to a friend, family member, or therapist about areas in which you feel unprepared. Practice with a friend so that you can feel more confident in handling a wide range of reactions. It might also be helpful to recall similar situations. What did you like about how you handled those? What do you wish you'd done differently?

Emotional Preparation

Though all the techniques so far are indirectly preparing for emotions by regulating your physical body and easing anxiety through logistical preparation, it can be helpful to directly prepare yourself emotionally as well. What emotions do you feel will come up in the conversation? How are you feeling right now? (Chapter 7 has some techniques for identifying your emotions.) What Automatic Thoughts might come up during the conversation that will cause the emotions you predict feeling? Are the thoughts true? Will your feelings be validated by the other person? How can you cope in the moment? Planning your self-care for after the conversation (see Chapter 10) will help you know you'll have time to process what comes up during the conversation.

Imagine if you were worried you'd feel angry during a conversation. Are the Automatic Thoughts of "they don't listen to me and therefore don't respect me" true? Being able to challenge these thoughts in the moment might help with lowering your anger enough to continue with the conversation, as can knowing you've got a kickboxing class later where you can really express your anger physically in a safe way!

Calming Down during Conversations

Calming techniques can be difficult to remember mid-conversation. I suggest that my clients practice calming techniques in many different types of conversations, so that the techniques become a habit rather than something to remember only in the moment. Practicing these skills in daily conversation allows you to have them at the forefront of your mind, well-practiced and ready to use! Below are some examples of calming techniques you can use during conversations.

Breathing.

While the other person is speaking, take deep breaths. Remember that long, slow, exhale from paced breathing? That is a great one to use mid-conversation, but be aware not to sound like you're sighing, as that can be interpreted negatively! Deep breathing is not only helpful to you, but also helps keep the other person calm. If you can stay calm, chances are the other person will stay calm as well, because we tend to mirror the behavior of others around us. Try it: take a slow deep breath when speaking with someone and see if they also take a slow deep breath without even knowing it.

Grounding.

Drinking water, preferably ice water, is a great way to stay present during an intense conversation. Take a sip and feel the water going down your throat. How does the bottle or glass feel in your hands? What does it look like? Does the ice make a sound in the glass? What does it taste like? Does the water have a smell? This is another way to drop into those five senses to help stay present and grounded during a conversation.

Slowing Down.

Speaking slowly and being mindful of what you are saying is a great way to stay calm. This also helps the receiver of the information stay calm, as they have more time to process and respond. If you find your rate of speech getting quicker, take a breath and slow down. Give the other person time to respond while you regroup.

Calming Down after Conversations

In Chapter 10 ("Practice Self-Care"), you'll learn more calming techniques for after conversations, but as I mentioned earlier, the calming and self-care techniques you plan to use post-conversation can be prepped before the conversation occurs.

Staying Calm in Spontaneous Conversations

As with setting personal goals, the more you use techniques during everyday conversations, the easier it will be to remember your skills when things happen unexpectedly. You can always access your breath during conversations. You can also ask for time to regulate (whether that means getting up for water, taking a moment to visit the restroom, or simply asking for a pause to walk outside). This may not always be possible, but it can be worth asking. (We'll look at this in more detail in Chapter 14 ("Setting Boundaries Skillfully").)

"But It's Really Hard to Stay Calm!"

Staying calm can be very, very difficult! We are emotional beings, and we are all capable of being angry, hurt, sad, or frustrated. These emotions are normal, and there are healthy ways to express and process them while still being able to communicate effectively. If you are having trouble staying "calm enough" during conversations, it might be time to ask yourself why.

Apply the cognitive model we discussed in the Introduction (page 3). Think about the situation, then about your reaction. Then go back and fill in your Automatic Thoughts. What were you thinking, assuming, predicting, and remembering? Are those thoughts accurate and true?

If you are still having trouble staying calm, explore with a therapist to get to the root of any personal blocks.

PRACTICE MAKES ~~PERFECT~~ EASIER

Choose one of the techniques suggested in this chapter for before or during conversations, and try to practice it before or during every single conversation you have in a day. The next day, choose a different technique. The more you practice, the more these will become second nature during all the conversations you have!

BOTTOM LINE

The point of calming down is not to lack emotion, but rather to be *calm enough* to have a productive, effective conversation. Use techniques for before, during, and after conversations to help achieve a *calm enough* state. Practice the calming techniques frequently so that they are easy to remember when spontaneous conversations occur, and so you can feel more calm and grounded overall!

Chapter 4

REMEMBER TO LISTEN

10 SKILLS OF COMMUNICATION

1. Set Personal Goals
2. Choose a Time, Place, and Platform
3. Calm Down (Enough)
4. **Remember to Listen**
5. State Common Goals
6. Validate
7. Describe
8. Find Solutions
9. Offer Positive Reinforcement
10. Practice Self-Care

INTRODUCTION

We've all felt unheard before. It's extremely frustrating! When we get frustrated, it becomes harder to communicate. Though listening skills can seem obvious, when we have something to say, sometimes we forget to *sit back and listen to see how what we've said has landed*. We forget that there is someone else involved in the conversation and keep forcing our point, or our reality, onto them. In this chapter, I'll explore the skills of listening, and you'll learn that when it comes to achieving your conversation goals, being quiet is just as important as what you say.

REMEMBERING TO LISTEN: WHY IT'S IMPORTANT

I love to talk—just ask anyone who has ever met me. However, one of the biggest lessons I've learned as a counselor—where it's my job to understand people—is the importance of listening. Listening is more than waiting your turn to speak; it's helping another person to feel heard, and it also allows you to understand how what you have said is being interpreted and understood by that person. Knowing how your reality is being perceived and understanding the other person's reality are crucial in being able to form your next statement, validate the other person, and come up with solutions to problems.

REMEMBERING TO LISTEN: HOW TO DO IT

Below are some "dos" and "don'ts" of good listening skills. These may seem obvious or juvenile, but oftentimes we easily forget these simple yet important skills!

Do:

- Make eye contact—at least a little. This can be uncomfortable, and too much eye contact can be intense; try two or three seconds of eye contact each time the other person speaks.
- Nod.
- Limit distractions (especially phones and other devices). Stop what you're doing and give the other person your full attention.
- Lean in a little.
- Unless you are walking, turn your body towards the other person (face, shoulders, torso, feet).
- Make sure you're in the same room (i.e., don't have a conversation from two separate spaces).
- Where appropriate, and only with consent, hold the other person's hand or do other non-sexual touch.

Don't:

* Say "mmm-hmm" or "yeah" while the other person is talking. This can seem like a good idea but can also backfire, with the result of them feeling rushed or like they're being interrupted.
* Finish the other person's sentences to show you understand.
* Use your vocal cords *at all* when listening.
* Make overexaggerated facial expressions as a nonverbal reaction before the other person is done speaking (this includes eye-rolling!).

Check Your Listening Skills

Sometimes you just want to help your conversation partner get there and finish their thought; you *know* what they're going to say so you interrupt and say it for them. Self-awareness around interrupting others can be a great way to up your conversation game and help keep conversations calm and concise.

Think about what Automatic Thoughts probably come up for the other person when you cut them off and interrupt. Does it seem like you care about what they're saying? Interrupting is a surefire way to derail conversations because it starts to bring up all sorts of emotional reactions that need to be attended to.

PRACTICE MAKES ~~PERFECT~~ EASIER

Choose one of the listening skills listed in the "Do" list above. Practice it in every conversation you have in a day. Then move to the next skill and do the same. You can also ask someone close to you which of the skills might benefit you the most. Ask them to remind you if, during a conversation you are on your phone, turning away, or leaving them feeling unheard. These corrections can be helpful in the moment for catching behavior and learning new skills.

If you struggle with interrupting, here's a technique to try: While another person is talking, press your index finger and thumb together. This is the position your mouth should be in—closed! Release your fingers when the other person is finished talking and it is your turn to speak. Doing a simple task like this (that no one else can see or needs to know about) will help focus your awareness on who is talking and help you stop interrupting. Over time, your awareness will increase, and you will no longer need this exercise!

BOTTOM LINE

Listening can seem simple, but it is often a forgotten part of communication. Take time to refresh yourself on how to be a good listener *before* you have a conversation. The importance of listening will become even more apparent as we explore validation (Chapter 6) and solution finding (Chapter 8).

Chapter 5

STATE COMMON GOALS

10 SKILLS OF COMMUNICATION

1. Set Personal Goals
2. Choose a Time, Place, and Platform
3. Calm Down (Enough)
4. Remember to Listen
5. **State Common Goals**
6. Validate
7. Describe
8. Find Solutions
9. Offer Positive Reinforcement
10. Practice Self-Care

INTRODUCTION

Now that we've gone over the four pre-conversation steps (set personal goals; choose a time, place, and platform; calm down (enough); and remember to listen), we are ready to start the conversation! When approaching a potentially emotionally intense exchange, it can be daunting to know how to start. Stating common goals is the most effective way to begin.

STATING COMMON GOALS: WHY IT'S IMPORTANT

Stating common goals at the beginning of a conversation reminds us *why we're having the conversation* and *why we're in the relationship*. It creates buy-in and motivates each person. One of the most important things that stating common goals does is align both people as a team against the problem, externalizing the problem from them and from the conversation. For example, the conversation is framed as someone's hurt feelings being the issue the team needs to solve together, rather than the issue being the person who is hurt.

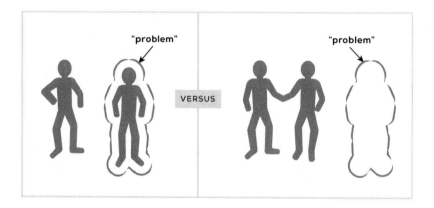

Stating common goals also indirectly tells the other person what the conversation is *not*. The conversation is not to shame, blame, or make anyone feel bad. As we learned at the beginning of this book, the conversation is also not to tell someone what to do or how to feel or to force them to change. Instead, stating common goals is a perfect way to start a conversation on a positive note; gives a good foundation from which to find solutions.

STATING COMMON GOALS: HOW TO DO IT

There are three steps to stating common goals: 1) find the goals; 2) keep it general; and 3) use positive language. Most of these steps can be done prior to the conversation, so that you have a general goal and positive language to use as a statement to start off the conversation.

1. Find the Goals

To identify common goals, ask yourself the following questions before the conversation:

- What are things you both want out of your interactions in general?
- Why are you in this relationship?
- Why are you in each other's lives?
- What is the desired outcome of this relationship in the short term? In the long term?
- How does the relationship benefit you both?
- What are things you both generally want in life?
- If you are a team, what is your mission?

Sometimes it can be surprising to remember that you and your conversation partner share common goals and are on the same team, because you've been arguing different realities for so long! But, in fact, you have things in common that you are both trying to achieve. Common goals are not necessarily about the specifics of the conversation itself but rather broad, general goals that you and the other person both have in common when it comes to your relationship. Common goals might even go beyond what any one individual needs, encompassing the purpose of the whole relationship.

2. Keep It General

This is extremely important. Common goals are very different from personal goals in that they're much less specific. Common goals are best if they're kept to general priorities or objectives *that you know the other person agrees with*. If the goal is something they disagree with, they might get defensive right out of the gate, which is not the best way to start a successful conversation! Look at the common goal examples below, and notice how they're different from the personal goals we discussed in Chapter 1. While it's important to be aware of both types of goals, the common goals are the ones to state at the beginning of the conversation.

Examples of Common Goals across Different Relationships

Romantic partnership/friendships

- We both want to be happy and help each other be happy.
- We both love each other and want to support one another.
- We want a peaceful life together where we both feel respected.

Co-parenting

- We both want our children to succeed and flourish.
- We hope our children grow up to be happy and healthy, and we will do anything we can to make that happen.

Family

- We both want to have peaceful family interactions and to spend time together.
- We both want to know about each other's lives.
- We love each other and want each other to be happy.

Roommates

- We both want to cohabitate peacefully.
- We both want to have a safe place to live.

Colleagues

* We both want the business to be successful and for things to run smoothly.

As you can see from these examples, common goals are very obvious statements that will get buy-in and maybe even some head nods from the other person, which will make both of you feel like a team that is working together. Notice they are general in the sense that they're not about the specific conversation goal but rather the larger relationship. However, they are more specific than just saying, "Remember, we're on the same team." This type of statement can seem empty unless you let them know *why* you're on the same team.

3. Use Positive Language

Now that you have identified your goals, stating them in positive language helps set the tone for the conversation. Check your language and frame your goals positively, so you're working toward what you both want instead of focusing on what you *don't* want. The following table compares negatively framed goals with positively framed goals. The goals in the right-hand column are the phrases you can use to open (potentially difficult or emotionally intense) conversations.

Negative-Language Goals	Positive-Language Goals
We both don't want to argue.	We want to have a more peaceful relationship. We want to be able to solve conflict efficiently.
We don't want our kids to be stressed.	We want our kids to be happy and healthy.
We don't want this project to fail.	We want this project to be successful.

Avoiding the "But"s

After opening a conversation by stating common goals, it is common to have the urge to say "but" before you move on to the next point. As much as possible, avoid using the word "but"—it can come across as invalidating the common goals you just stated.

For example, a phrase like "We love each other and want each other to be happy, but . . ." implies that the next statement you are going to make will contradict the common goal you just stated, which is the opposite of what you're trying to achieve! Leave out the word "but" altogether and instead use the word "and," or just start your next statement without the "but."

"We love each other and want each other to be happy. And you see the situation in this way. . . ."

"We love each other and want each other to be happy. You see the situation in this way. . . ."

This "no buts" rule is applied to all transitions—between stating common goals and validating, and between validating and describing.

> PRACTICE MAKES ~~PERFECT~~ EASIER

Think about all the people you interact with daily. Write down their names. Now, next to each name, write one or more common goals you share with that person. Keep them general and challenge yourself to use positive language! Feel free to state them in everyday conversation and see what the reaction is. Even if you are not headed toward a difficult conversation, stating common goals can be a great stand-alone skill to use to remind people of your shared goals and values, creating more connection and understanding.

BOTTOM LINE

Stating common goals to start a conversation can be a great alternative to "ripping the Band-Aid off" or "coming in hot," as a lot of us tend to do when beginning difficult conversations! Starting a conversation with positively phrased common goals will remind the other person why you are having the conversation and also will create buy-in to listening and coming up with solutions, if needed. Stating common goals means making some assumptions, so go with large, overarching goals that you are fairly certain are true for both parties. Think about these before your conversation, and check that your language is framed positively. Starting the conversation as an aligned team, rather than two people "against" each other, will set you up for more success!

Chapter 6

VALIDATE

10 SKILLS OF COMMUNICATION

1. Set Personal Goals
2. Choose a Time, Place, and Platform
3. Calm Down (Enough)
4. Remember to Listen
5. State Common Goals
6. **Validate**
7. Describe
8. Find Solutions
9. Offer Positive Reinforcement
10. Practice Self-Care

INTRODUCTION

Welcome to the most important aspect of communication, and the most vital skill you'll learn in this book! You may have heard of validating (also known as reflecting or having empathy) before. Validation provides the connection and understanding that is necessary and so often craved in communication.

However, despite its importance, validation often gets skipped in conversations because it's difficult! People either just don't know how to do it, or other urges (like describing one's own reality) take over. In this chapter, I will make a case for why validation not only benefits the person receiving it but is also *helpful to the person doing the validating*. You'll learn various ways to find people's realities and then reflect and validate those realities. I'll also address the common urges, blocks, and resistances that I often see getting in the way of validation. Of all the skills you'll learn in this book, validating is the one that'll get you closest to understanding others and being understood yourself!

VALIDATING: WHY IT'S IMPORTANT

Providing validation is a way to show someone you understand their reality and that you can accept that it's different from your own reality. Validation is helpful to the other person because it helps them feel understood in their reality. While this helpfulness can seem obvious, what might be less obvious is that validation is equally, if not more, helpful to you. There are three reasons why validating someone else is helpful to you:

1. It disarms defensiveness.

Validation disarms defensiveness in the other person, which creates space for you to state your reality (which comes next). If you've already shown you understand the other person, they are far less likely to come in and defend their reality. You'll be able to move the conversation forward, rather than getting caught up in a defense-of-realities cycle.

2. It models good behavior.

Remember the golden rule—treat others the way you want to be treated? Validating someone else models the behavior you want to see when it's your turn to describe your reality. During validation, you'll be using patience and listening skills (see Chapter 4), and getting curious about the other person's perspective. You'll be working hard to make them feel understood.

3. It helps you actually understand the other person.

We often project our own perspective onto others and assume that we know what they're thinking or feeling. When done properly, validation avoids projection and assumptions and ensures you fully understand where the other person is coming from, which is a vital part of connecting and being on the same page. When you understand someone, it is a lot easier to find solutions to problems, stay calm, and work together as a team.

Now that you know why validation is important, let's talk about how to do it (properly).

VALIDATING: HOW TO DO IT

Validating someone's reality has two steps: identifying their reality, then validating it. These steps are broken down below. When exploring other people's realities, you really want to focus on the emotions that are going on, because that will create a deeper sense of understanding and connection than just knowing their surface reality. Sure, you can understand that they see things a certain way, but how do they *feel* about it?

1. Identifying the Other Person's Reality

First, you must do your best to find out what the other person's reality might be and how they feel about the situation. Here is where the skills learned in Chapter 4 ("Remember to Listen") come in handy! This piece can be tricky because you will be making tentative assumptions about someone's experience, yet it's the best way to show you are at least *trying* to understand. Below are some clues that will help you best conceptualize another person's reality.

Clue #1 to Their Reality: Emotion Words

The other person might have already told you how they feel by using emotion words. "I'm frustrated." "I'm upset." "I'm nervous." Common emotions include fear, anger, anxiety, happiness, sadness, or love. See the Table of Emotion Words in Appendix II (page 262) for a comprehensive list of emotion words to look out for.

Clue #2 to Their Reality: Nonverbal Cues

Along with paying attention to the words they use, another way to pick up on the other person's reality is their expression of nonverbal cues, as listed in the following table.

Type of Expression	Example of Expression	What It Might Mean
Facial expressions	Smiling	Happy or in agreement with what's going on
	Frowning	Disapproving, concerned, or angry
	Furrowing brows	Confused
Body language	Crossed arms or turning away	Defensive
	Turning toward	Open, understanding
Volume	Yelling	Angry, frustrated, misunderstood, unheard, or overwhelmed
	Mumbling	Uncertain or afraid
Behavior	Crying	Sad
	Fidgeting	Nervous, bored
	Avoiding eye contact	Anxious, ashamed, or perhaps even respectful
Tone	Sarcastic	Disrespectful, threatened
	Genuine	Accepting, happy, secure, or supportive

Clue #3 to Their Reality: Explanation of the Situation

If the other person has shared a situation that you want to validate, in order (in order to) to further understand their reality, you can ask yourself the following questions:

- Put yourself in their shoes. How might you feel if you were them?
- What's another way to look at this situation?
- What are their possible Automatic Thoughts about the situation?
- Have you been in a similar situation before? Which side were you on? How did both parties feel?
- How might they interpret this situation if they assume your best intentions?
- How might they interpret this situation if they assume your worst intentions?
- If you were on the other side of this situation, how would you interpret it?

If you have time before a conversation to prepare, really take the time to think about the answers to the questions above—or even ask a third party for more help in understanding different viewpoints. If you don't have time to prepare, do your best to remind yourself of other perspectives in the moment.

FINDING REALITIES: PRACTICE MAKES ~~PERFECT~~ EASIER

Below are four ways to practice and hone the skill of identifying someone else's reality. These are great to do before difficult conversations if you have the time to prepare. They are also great exercises to practice on a situation that you don't intend to talk about, as it will help you get better at putting yourself in someone else's shoes or reality, understand them better, and be able to access this skill when spontaneous conversations arise.

1. Daily Routine

Imagine the other person waking up in the morning. What was their routine? Close your eyes and imagine what they did between opening their eyes and speaking with you, and how they might think and feel in each moment. Then focus on your interaction with them. Given what you now think about their day, how might they interpret what has happened? What might their Automatic Thoughts be? Notice any difference in how they might interpret the situation and your own interpretation of the situation given your short-term histories. For instance, when you accidentally spilled their coffee, might they be thinking, "Great, another thing going wrong today," because they've already stubbed their toe on their way out the door and then missed the bus? Or might they be thinking, "Ah well, I'll just grab another one; this is still the best day ever!" because they just won $10,000 in the lottery the night before?

2. Life Timeline

This is similar to the Daily Routine exercise, but much broader: you're creating a whole life timeline. You probably won't know every detail of the other person's life, but use what you do know. How did they end up here? What obstacles, successes, challenges, skills, resources, and supports do they have? What is shaping their Automatic Thoughts? Once you've imagined their life as best as you can up until the present time, add in the Daily Routine exercise.

3. Bird's-Eye View

If you are wondering about different interpretations of a certain situation, another great way to find someone's reality is to replay the situation from a bird's-eye view. Replay the situation in your mind as if you were watching a movie; you can even imagine your favorite actors in the roles. Seeing the situation from a third-party perspective can help remove your own biases and find other realities, assumptions, and interpretations.

4. Instant Replay

Think of a conversation that escalated or that confused you. Now replay it from the other person's viewpoint. You can even have the conversation in a mirror and watch yourself, or record a video of yourself repeating the conversation. This can be uncomfortable, because we often have a skewed view of what we look like, sound like, and how we come across. Ever heard your voice in a recording? Sounds a lot different than we expect! That said, be gentle on yourself.

Asking for Clarification

If emotion words, nonverbal cues, and an explanation of the situation still leave you unsure of the other person's reality, you can directly ask them to explain more:

* Can you tell me a bit more about what happens for you when you see that I haven't done the dishes?

This is a great example of a question that is phrased to invite a full answer. If possible, avoid using closed questions (questions that can be answered with a yes or no). Closed questions often start with the words *do, did, are,* or *is.* For example:

* "*Do* you feel mad?"
* "*Did* you feel hurt?"
* "*Are* you going to . . . ?"
* "*Is* this going to . . . ?"

Leading questions are another type of question to avoid. Leading questions push someone toward an answer you are expecting, or in a particular direction, using assumptions from your reality. These assumptions then impose your reality onto the other person, and as we have learned, that imposition leads to defensiveness.

- "Are you okay?" (This closed question leads the person into thinking about if they're okay or not. A yes/no answer will not give you any information other than whether they're okay.)
- "Why are you upset?" (This open but leading question still implies that they are upset, leading them to think about this emotion only. It is also imposing being upset onto them, which might elicit defensiveness: "I'm not upset!")
- "You're not hurt, are you?" (This closed question has a very obvious intended outcome—for the person to agree they are not hurt! This is not allowing space for the person to feel whatever they feel in their reality. There is more on how to handle unintentionally hurting someone later in the book.)

Instead, try open-ended questions or statements to gather more information. Open-ended questions usually include words such as *how, what,* and *why,* as in:

- "*How* are you feeling?"
- "Could you tell me a bit about *what's* going on for you right now?"
- "I'm curious about *how* you're feeling right now."
- "Could you tell me *why* you're crying?"

Being aware of the words you're using will take practice but is worth it because it minimizes the chance of defensiveness derailing the conversation. Open-ended questions will also help you to better understand the other person's reality—a key component of validation. When in doubt, an open-ended question that will usually cut right to someone's emotions is, "How are you feeling?"

2. Validating Their Reality

Now that you've done some detective work and have a good sense of what might be going on for the other person in their reality, it's time to actually validate it! Validation can come in a few different forms: reflections, empathetic reflections, and using tentative leads with empathetic reflections.

Validation through Reflections

Validation is simple (though not always easy). One of the simplest forms it can take is that of reflecting—saying back the content of what the other person said to you. This shows that you have heard what they said and that you accept and understand their reality.

- "You're having a really rough day."
- "The test didn't go so well today."
- "Your best friend just told you she's having a baby!"

Use some of the words that they've used, but try not to repeat verbatim, or you risk sounding insincere or parrot-like.

Validation through Empathetic Reflections

If you want to take validation a step further and demonstrate understanding of the other person's feelings as well as their reality, then an empathetic reflection can be helpful. Empathetic reflections include a reflection plus some emotional vocabulary. See the Table of Emotion Words in Appendix II (page 262) for help with this, or use the emotion word they've *already* used to explain the situation.

- "You're feeling really tired and burned out."
- "Anxiety is really strong for you right now."
- "You got news you're really excited and happy about!"

Validation Using Tentative Leads with Empathetic Reflections

A tentative lead can be helpful in not imposing your assumptions of reality onto the other person. This is extremely useful if you feel the person tends to get defensive or you're not sure if you've got the right emotion for them. Tentative leads can take the form of:

- "It sounds like . . ."
- "It seems like . . ."
- "I'm getting the sense that . . ."
- "That probably felt . . ."
- "That possibly was . . ."
- "It looks like that is . . ."

The next table contains more examples of types of reflections and what they look like when used in conversation.

Tone

Tone is a very important part of how we communicate; however, it is difficult to teach tone in a book! My best advice is that people will usually be able to uncover your motive or underlying thoughts through the tone you use. When it comes to validation, I sometimes see people new to this skill just "getting it over with," and you can really tell. Though they might be spot-on when it comes to the language they choose, their tone is way off, and it's obvious they're just getting over the validation hurdle so that they can get on to describing their own reality. Whether you are sincere or are placating someone, they will pick up on that in your tone. That's why the skills in this book are meant for people with the true goal of having successful, reciprocal relationships. Keep your common goals in mind when speaking to help you stay sincere. Remember how and why validation is helpful to you both. Have sincere curiosity, be patient, and know that your turn will be coming soon!

Situation	Reflection	Empathetic Reflection with Emotion Words	Empathetic Reflection with Tentative Leads
Your partner's car didn't start in the morning.	So, you were sitting in the car, and it was making that sound and not starting at all!	So, you were sitting in the car, getting really *frustrated* that it wouldn't start, then you were *scared* you were going to be late for work. That is a very *stressful* morning!	So, you were sitting in the car, *probably* getting really frustrated that it wouldn't start, then you were scared you were going to be late for work. *I'm getting the sense that* you've had a very stressful morning!
Your friend was just broken up with by text message.	Your partner just decided it was time to leave and decided to tell you that via text!	It's *heartbreaking* that they decided to leave and *disrespectful* that they did it over text.	*That sounds* heartbreaking that they decided to leave, and *maybe it felt* disrespectful that they did it over text.
A roommate or partner is upset with you for not doing the dishes.	You came home and the dishes weren't done, even though I said I would do them.	You are *angry* that you came home after a long, *exhausting* day to find I hadn't done the dishes.	*Seems like* you're feeling angry because I didn't do the dishes when I said I would. *That was probably* an exhausting end to your long day.
Your teenager had a bad day at school.	You tripped in gym class, and everyone laughed; then you also got a poor grade on a math test.	It was really *embarrassing* to trip in gym class, and then on top of that you got the math test back, which was so *discouraging*. What a *frustrating* day!	*It sounds like* it was really embarrassing to trip in gym class, and then, on top of that, you got the math test back, and *that sounds like* it was so discouraging. *Seems like* you had a frustrating day!

If Someone's Reality Seems Confusing and Contradictory

Even if we are aware and accepting that other people have different realities than ours, those other realities can still seem extremely confusing and even contradictory. Here's the rule of thumb I tell my clients: *if you're confused about someone else's thoughts or behavior, chances are* they *are confused as well.* They have probably not taken the time to be aware of their thoughts or beliefs about a situation, or to think about how they are being interpreted by others. To manage a situation where someone is saying or doing things that don't make sense, validate that confusion for them:

- "It seems like you might be confused."
- "Sounds like you're feeling a whole bunch of different things right now!"
- "I'm getting the sense you can't choose between [action 1] and [action 2]."
- "This is a tough situation! How has it been for you, figuring out what you want to do?"

In addition, you can validate each thing they've done or said, instead of attempting to validate the situation as a whole. They may be thinking out loud; ask them to describe to you how they're feeling so you can understand where they're at now. Use the listening skills you learned in Chapter 4, and be on the lookout for any emotion words that are used.

If You Get Their Reality Wrong

When trying to find and validate someone's reality, we are still making assumptions, and sometimes we assume wrongly. That's okay! If you don't get it right, usually the person will correct you. If they do, note the emotion words, nonverbal cues, or situations they describe, and validate those! You can also get curious and ask open-ended questions, or simply ask, "Did I get that right?"

I volunteered at a crisis hotline for a year and a half, an experience in which I answered phone calls from people who were in a high level of distress and often having suicidal thoughts and urges. In my training for the hotline, we learned about the power of validation; however, it was obvious that a lot of us were extremely scared of "getting it wrong" and creating even more distress! Luckily for us, we learned from our teachers and callers that this was not usually the case—the more likely scenario was that we'd guess an emotion incorrectly and then a caller would correct us:

Hotline Operator: "Sounds like you're feeling really upset about that."

Caller: "Hmmm, I'm not so much upset, more like worried."

This interaction usually didn't lead to a disconnect, and we were able to move on with the conversation:

Hotline Operator: "So you're feeling worried and anxious about what will happen?"

Caller: "Yeah, exactly."

There may be rare cases when, if you don't get your validation right, the other person gets defensive or agitated:

Person A: "I'm getting the sense that you're jealous of her."

Person B: "How could you think I'm jealous of her?"

Person A: "So that situation sounds like it caused anger for you."

Person B: "Why would you think I'm the kind of person who would get angry at that? Is that what you think of me?"

Person A: "Seems like you're feeling upset about the situation."

Person B: "No. I'm hurt, and I'm angry! Can't you see that!?"

If this happens, validate how they're feeling about the incorrect assumption.

- "You're angry and offended that I asked if you were jealous."
- "It sounds like you're hurt that I implied you were angry, because being angry about that would mean you're a bad person or something."
- "You're hurt and angry!"

You can always go back to validating the main issue, do another reflection in the form of a summary to make sure you're on the same page, or ask for more clarification. This also potentially a situation where the person just needs some time and space to gather their thoughts, so you can always offer that as well.

You Have Their Emotion Right, but They're Still Defensive

Sometimes people will really resist admitting to feeling a certain emotion. Anger is a popular one, and jealousy is another. There is sometimes shame or other "weaknesses" associated with these feelings, so resistance to admitting those emotions occurs.

For example, think of someone screaming "I'm not angry!" when they really seem like they are angry. They probably *don't want to be angry*, and that's okay! Ask them to describe how they feel and then validate their reality. If they *seem* really angry to you, they might be angry and not ready to admit it, but they also might not be angry at all and instead be feeling a different emotion that you missed. The great thing is that is doesn't matter if they're angry or not. Validate what they are saying they feel because *the point of validating is not to get their emotion correct, but to get their reality correct.* In their reality, they aren't angry, so validate that (even if in your reality they are acting really angry).

BEHAVIORAL AND MENTAL BLOCKS TO VALIDATION

I've explained how important validation is and how it creates the connection and understanding we all want. Why aren't we all doing it all the time, then? In the next two sections, I'll explore common behavioral urges that get in the way of validation, and I'll list some common areas of mental resistance that are faced when trying to validate others.

Behavioral Urges That Block Validation

Sometimes we have urges to do things in a conversation that are extremely well-intentioned but can come off as minimizing or invalidating to someone's reality, especially their feelings. For example, problem-solving, cheerleading, storytelling, minimizing, and assuming are all examples of tools we can use to connect, but without validating *first*, these natural reactions have the opposite effect and can come across as invalidating. Once someone feels invalidated, they can get defensive, or even shut down. I'll go through each of these urges that block validation in more detail and show how some of them can be useful when combined with validation skills.

1. Problem-Solving

- "Why don't you just [solution idea]?"
- "Have you tried [solution idea]?"
- "You should [solution idea]."

Problem-solving is an extremely common urge, and probably the one I most often see getting in the way of validation. If someone we care about is in distress, we want to help them—so we offer solutions! Although this is very well-intentioned, the other person might interpret it as you thinking their problem is minor or that they're stupid for not trying your proposed solution, which creates (or adds to) frustration.

You might be thinking to yourself, "How is validating them helping with their problem? Especially with the example about a car not starting—how is validation going to start their car? They need help to solve their problem, not understand it, right!?" You are 100 percent correct that they need help, but *validation is setting the stage for the person to feel understood and thus to be open to accepting help.* After some quick validation, you can then move on to solution-finding. The urge to problem-solve isn't wrong, but the other person will be a lot more open to your proposed solutions if you've first demonstrated that you *understand.* For example:

- "Wow, it's stressful and frustrating that the car won't start. Have you tried calling a shared ride service to drive you to work?"

In the next chapter, we'll talk more about finding solutions to problems you face together with another person.

2. Cheerleading

- "You can do it! It will be okay!"
- "You can get through it!"

If we see someone we care about having a tough time, we want to cheer them on and reassure them. However, jumping to cheerleading right away does not show that you understand or that you believe the other person's feelings are important. In fact, it can feel extremely invalidating! Instead, try some cheerleading *after* empathetic reflections, like in the examples below:

- "This is a really stressful and sad time for you right now, but I know you can get through it."
- "It's really painful for you to be in this situation, but it won't last forever."

3. Storytelling

- "The same thing happened to me once."
- "I've been there!"
- "Oh man, I know what you mean; that happened to a friend of mine. . . ."
- "I know how you feel, once, I . . ."

Who doesn't love a good story? I am a huge fan. Storytelling is often done to show we can empathize ("See, I've been in the same position before too!") or to offer advice ("See what I did when this happened to me?").

Again, the intentions are very pure, but telling a story about yourself or someone else doesn't show that you understand. While it might be an attempt to bond, it distracts from the other person's feelings.

Giving advice by showing how you handled a situation (whether it was a success or not) can be helpful. However, as with the previous examples, it's best done after an empathetic reflection. For example:

- "That sounds really frustrating that your car won't start. I was once stuck in an intersection, and it was really embarrassing and frustrating! I called a tow truck, and they came to get me."

If you choose to use storytelling with validation, keep in mind that it's helpful to give the other person the full time and space they need to tell their story *and* to be validated *before* moving on to talking about yourself or giving advice through storytelling.

It's also important to note that sometimes it's not appropriate to talk about yourself when validating. For counselors, "self-disclosure" (a fancy word for talking about your personal life) is something we use very deliberately or avoid altogether. Think about what it would be like if you went in to see a counselor to help you with your problems and all they did was talk about themselves. Keep this in mind next time someone close to you comes to you with a problem. They probably want you to just listen.

This holds especially true if you are in a position of power (boss, manager, teacher, etc.), as personal information can skew the power dynamic, be inappropriate, or cause the person discomfort in feeling like they *must* take your advice. Use your best judgment as to whether personal stories about yourself or others will help you achieve your goals in the conversation. Telling a story to a coffee shop employee about how you prepped for an interview is appropriate, but empathizing with that same employee about your sexual preferences is not appropriate.

And no matter the situation, if you are telling a story about someone else, make sure you have consent from the other person to share their story, or take out identifying information and keep it general.

4. Minimizing

- "You're feeling a little stressed about that."
- "You've got a tiny bit of sadness because of that."

In everyday conversations, phrases like "a little" or "a tiny bit" assume that you know the quantity of that emotion, and that it's not that bad. The other person might feel bad or angry that you think they are overreacting. Minimizing can be infuriating to the receiver!

Instead of using minimizing language, try reflecting the emotion without describing the amount of that emotion:

Minimizing Phrase	Non-Minimizing Phrase
You're feeling a little stressed about that.	You're feeling stressed about that!
You're a tiny bit sad.	You're sad.

5. Assuming

- "I understand."
- "I get it."
- "I hear you."
- "I know. . . ."

Such statements are meant to let someone know you understand them, and in a casual conversation they sometimes go over very well. However, although very well-intentioned like the rest of the urges, assuming statements can sometimes *not* be well received because they're vague: they do not actually show the other person you accurately understand, get it, or hear them. Instead, they focus on you and your reality and make a huge assumption that you *do* understand, get, or hear the other person.

For example, when someone is upset about their car not starting, a simple "I get it" might assume they're frustrated and don't know how to solve the problem. It might completely miss that they are extremely sad because being broken down on the side of the road reminded them of when they lost a friend in a car accident. Assuming statements miss out on an important reason we validate others: to make sure we understand them!

Another issue: if you use shortcut assumption statements, you miss the chance to model talking about emotions. This may mean that when it's your turn to talk, the other person will be less likely to inquire about your emotions or less likely to work to actually understand, get, or hear you. This can perpetuate a culture of misunderstanding and a fear of expressing emotions. Instead of these assumption statements, use empathetic reflections to show that you feel comfortable talking about emotions and are trying to understand. Talking about emotions *can* be uncomfortable! Yet, with practice it becomes easier, and you can know for sure that you understand others.

Prefacing a validation with "I know" is another piece of assuming language that, although well-intentioned, can backfire. The person saying this is most likely trying to show empathy, and that they understand, or "know," how the other person feels. But on the receiving end, "I know" can seem presumptuous and lead to defensiveness: For example:

Person A: "I know it's hard for you to be at school without your mobile phone."

Person B: "Do you? Did they use these phones when you were a kid?"

Instead, just remove the "I know," and try an empathetic reflection, perhaps with a tentative lead:

* "It's hard for you to be at school without your phone."
* "It sounds like it's really hard for you to be at school without your phone."

These statements validate the speaker and show that you understand how they feel. In particular, the second statement shows that *you don't as-*

sume you know 100 percent how they feel. Even if you've had a very similar experience, it's usually safer to avoid "I know," as we all interpret things very differently (remember The Dress?). Instead, show you understand by using reflections and empathetic reflections.

Mental Resistances That Block Validation

Now that you're aware of the common behavioral urges that block validation, let's take a look at some mental, or psychological, blocks that create resistance to validation.

1. "I don't agree with them."

This the most common issue that gets in the way of validation, and I've touched on it before—*validating someone's reality is not the same as agreeing with it*. But sometimes, in our minds, we think that validating does mean agreeing, and our ego won't let us give in to agreeing with something that is not true in our reality!

You can tell that this worry about agreeing with someone is coming up when, as someone is talking, phrases like these pop up in your mind:

- "They shouldn't feel that way" (or other "should/shouldn't" language)
- "They just don't get it."
- "They're wrong."
- "That's not true."
- "No."

These statements reflect some stubbornness around seeing other perspectives. If you find yourself in this position and want to explore how to better accept another person's reality, think about why the resistance happens and how to manage it effectively.

Often it can feel as though, by validating someone else, we're "giving in" or "agreeing" with the other person, or even (gasp) losing the argument. Validating someone can threaten our own reality, and we are very protective of our realities! These are common, valid fears.

In order to keep your own reality intact, and therefore help you feel better about offering validation, think back to the examples of validating statements you learned about earlier in this chapter. Validating statements typically have the word "you" in them. You are *describing* someone else's reality; you are *not* phrasing their reality as fact. Take a look at these two statements:

1. "So you think The Dress is white and gold."
2. "The Dress is white and gold."

The first example is a great one of how I would validate someone else. They see The Dress as white and gold, and I'm showing them I understand that. If I had instead said the second statement—"The Dress is white and gold"—it would feel terrible to me because that's literally not how I see it! I would be very reluctant to make a statement like that because, in my reality, it is completely untrue that the dress is gold and white.

Again, accepting someone's reality is not agreeing with it! You don't agree they "should" feel the way they do, and that's understandable. But in their reality, in their worldview, it's valid for them to feel how they are feeling. To them it is understandable and acceptable, and it makes sense. And that's all you need to acknowledge.

2. "I feel bad that they feel bad."

You feel guilt or shame that your actions were interpreted incorrectly, and you don't want to acknowledge the accidental pain you've caused. Managing these emotions can be difficult, but it can help to know that the best thing you can do in instances of mistakes, misinterpretation, or miscommunication is to empathize with the other person and their reality. Validating is not admitting that you had malicious intentions—it's showing you understand that something was taken the wrong way. Being humble and admitting you (unintentionally and accidentally) caused someone pain is a huge sign of emotional maturity and will benefit your relationships immensely. In Chapter 11 ("Stories of the Ten Skills in Action"), you'll learn more about managing unexpected reactions.

3. "I'm afraid that validating their 'bad' emotion will make them feel 'worse.'"

This is a common fear around validation. Saying "you feel sad" might make them sadder, and you don't want that! You want them to be happy! Practicing validation is helpful in squashing this mistaken notion. Remember my story from the crisis hotline? Letting someone know you understand the way they feel will *not* intensify their emotion! It will help them feel understood and connected.

4. "I just don't care about their issue."

Maybe you don't care about the topic the other person is bringing up. You think it's silly and therefore you shouldn't validate it. However, validation is not about *your* intentions or priorities. It's about the other person's feelings. Remember that they have a whole life of different and unique experiences and ways of looking at things. Rather than being rigid in your mindset, try to open up and explore how the other person sees the world.

For example, my partner really doesn't care about the dishwasher being loaded properly; he thinks it's silly to talk about or get upset over. However, I remind him that it makes me feel like my time and our energy bill aren't respected when he doesn't load it properly and we have to re-wash items. The dishwasher is not the point here; the distressing feelings I experience are what need attention. People might have feelings about things like dishwashers that just don't make sense to you. But think about The Dress; we all see the world differently!

5. "I don't want to condone or reinforce their behavior."

It may seem that you are condoning behavior by validating it, or you may think it's counterproductive to validate an emotion like anger. However, validation does not reward behavior or cause it to intensify; it simply shows that you understand the behavior. Validation is also just one aspect of a conversation; describing (see Chapter 7) can come later, and this is the time you can let someone know that their behavior has negative consequences. Again, accepting and validating are not agreeing with a behavior, or saying it's correct.

6. "It's not fair that their reality gets attention first, when I'm the one doing all the work."

It can be frustrating to feel like you're the one doing all the "heavy lifting" of communication. But don't forget that while validation can seem like it's all about the other person, it benefits you as well. Validation preemptively shuts down defensiveness, and that will give you a more open, accepting space to describe your own reality and be understood.

Remembering that you will soon get your turn might be helpful in managing frustrations. You can also remind yourself of your own personal goals for the conversation, as well as your common goals, as motivation to validate. Another option for managing the potential frustration of validating the other person first is to give them a copy of this book or to lend them yours! If others learn effective skills, you'll feel less alone in doing all the communication work.

7. "I really just don't want to validate."

I've made the best case I can for why validation is an extremely important part of a productive conversation, and why it's valuable both to you and the other person. Here's my case again in list form.

Validation is useful because:

1. It shuts down the other person's defensiveness before it even begins.
2. It helps you really understand the other person, which is helpful later when finding solutions, and helpful in the present moment to keep the other person calm.
3. It models the behavior you want to see from the other person.
4. It helps the other person feel good because they are understood.

Trying validation, and observing what happens, can often be the best way to see and understand how powerful it can be. If you want to try validating but just can't seem to move past the blocks in your way, this could be a great topic to discuss with a therapist. They might have better insights about your resistance to validating others and what this means to you.

PRACTICE MAKES ~~PERFECT~~ EASIER

Validation may seem awkward or unnatural at first. You might even be fighting off some of the behavioral and mental blocks previously discussed. In order to get more comfortable, try using one validating phrase per interaction. Start with simple reflections at first. Once you feel comfortable with those, move to adding emotion words, then add some tentative leads, and perhaps guess at some deeper emotions. It can be helpful to take a photo of the Table of Emotion Words (page 262) and keep it in your phone for easy reference. If any of this feels uncomfortable at first, that's a natural part of the learning process.

Here's a validation analogy that might help this make more sense: I was a synchronized swimmer for over more than ten years. At one point in my life, I could do "flat splits." In a flat split, no light can pass between you and the ground because both legs are flat on the floor, in a perfect split position. When stretching my splits at home one night, my sister looked at me and asked me to teach her how to do them. I told her it can't actually be taught. You simply need to practice and stretch a little more, day after day, until you reach a flat split. The practice and stretching is uncomfortable at first, but soon flat splits feel as comfortable as sitting in a chair or in any other position.

Validation is just like the splits; it can be uncomfortable at first, but it gets easier and easier with time, as long as you continue to do it. And just like the splits, validation skills need to be maintained. Finding ways to validate other people helps it become easier and more natural. Practice will also help you understand others and help them to feel understood, which is a very, very powerful outcome of communication!

I've already mentioned practicing a lot in this book, and (spoiler alert!) I will continue to mention it a lot more. These communication skills really do need practice. I have seen clients go from fumbling to find emotion words and taking huge pauses in the middle of sentences to having natural, flowing, spot-on validation statements. Their perseverance and practice paid off big time! And it can for you too!

When It's Validating, and When It's Describing

In my work with couples, I see a lot of arguments. A big tip-off that two people are caught up in defense of realities is that they are not validating; they are only describing. You'll learn more about describing in the next chapter, but for now all you need to know is that descriptive statements usually start with "I," and validating statements, as we've learned, usually contain "you." Below is an example of two people arguing because they are only describing, not validating:

Person A: "I was really hurt by that."

Person B: "I didn't mean to hurt you!"

Person A: "Well, I still felt hurt."

Person B: "Well, I felt hurt too!"

. . . and on it goes. Or another example:

Person A: "I thought you were supposed to pick up the kids."

Person B: "I thought you were supposed to remind me."

Person A: "I was already so stressed that day. Did you remember I had that meeting?"

Person B: "I had obviously forgotten, and I thought we'd agreed you'd remind me!"

Person A: "Well, I didn't!"

. . . and on it goes.

No one in these examples is validating; there is just a lot of describing going on. This points to both people feeling misunderstood. They are caught up in events, in "what happened" (in other words, whose reality is "correct"), and are not getting to the goal of the conversation. In the example about picking up the kids, the goal was to feel understood and find solutions so the situation wouldn't be repeated. Neither of those goals can be achieved, though, until someone starts a phrase or sentence with "you" and uses emotion words to describe how they're most likely feeling.

Speaker A: "I thought you were supposed to pick up the kids." (describe)

Speaker B: "You were confused and shocked when you heard I didn't pick them up." (validate)

Speaker A: "Yes."

Speaker B: "That must have been really frustrating for you, especially since you had that big meeting." (validate)

Speaker A: "Yes."

Speaker B: "It seems there was a miscommunication. What do you think we can do next time so it's clearer for both of us? Do you want to try writing things down on the calendar?" (See Chapter 8 for more about finding solutions.)

In this example, Speaker B puts aside their need to describe and instead defuses the argument using validation.

If you are in a relationship where there is a lot of arguing or conflict, try this the next time things escalate; it might just be the key to breaking the cycle. Avoid starting sentences with "I" and instead use the word "you" plus some emotion words that the other person is most likely feeling.

BOTTOM LINE

Validating another person helps them—and you! It's really a win-win. Now you have the skills to explore and understand someone else's reality, verbally validate it, and manage blocks and resistance that might get in the way. Having the patience to put describing your own reality aside for a moment and first validate the other person will pay dividends when it's your turn to be heard. Later in the book you will see how validation is often the go-to skill for when conversations don't go as planned; when in doubt, validate, validate, validate!

Chapter 7

DESCRIBE

10 SKILLS OF COMMUNICATION

1. Set Personal Goals
2. Choose a Time, Place, and Platform
3. Calm Down (Enough)
4. Remember to Listen
5. State Common Goals
6. Validate
7. **Describe**
8. Find Solutions
9. Offer Positive Reinforcement
10. Practice Self-Care

INTRODUCTION

Describing: this might be the chapter you've been waiting for—when you finally get to explain *your* side of things! You've done all the conversation prep, aligned yourself with your conversation partner through common goals, and helped the other person to open up using validation. All of this has been valuable preparation for the seventh communication skill of describing. In this chapter, you'll learn what describing is and how to do it (including how to increase your emotional awareness). Examples, tips, and troubleshooting (for instance, how to answer when someone responds to your describing with "You shouldn't feel that way") will help you bring the describing skill to life.

DESCRIBING: WHY IT'S IMPORTANT

This aspect of communication is important because it conveys *your* reality—which is just as valid as anyone else's! Describing (perhaps with the intent to feel understood or validated) is a common personal goal for conversations as we often want to feel heard and understood by others.

DESCRIBING: HOW TO DO IT

Just like validating, describing is a two-step process. First, you must be aware of how you feel (Find Your Emotions), and second, you must verbalize and communicate those emotions (Communicate How You Feel). And again, just like validating, in describing there is a lot of focus on emotions; connection comes best from being understood emotionally.

1. Find Your Emotions

If you aren't aware of how you're feeling, no one else will be. This is a great opportunity to practice getting to know yourself! Building your personal emotional vocabulary and emotional intelligence helps you understand your own feelings so that you can get better at describing them.

Here is a five-part exercise I often give to clients who need help getting to know their emotions. It helps with emotional vocabulary—the words that you use to describe your current state—as well as the physical aspect of emotions, or the sensations. We call them *feelings* because they show up physically (we literally "feel" them), although we're often unaware of that.

1. Ask yourself how you feel.

If needed, use the Table of Emotion Words (page 262). Be as specific as you can; try to find one word that pinpoints how you're feeling. You can even look up words and their meanings until you find the one that fits. Just as with realities and Automatic Thoughts, we don't want to label emotions as right or wrong, good or bad, healthy or unhealthy. Instead, try your best to take on a mindful, nonjudgmental approach to noticing. That's all. Notice how you feel. Say, "Hmmm, that's interesting," and pick a word.

2. Ask yourself how the emotion is showing up in your body.

Often we are cut off from our senses, but recognizing the feeling associated with an emotion can be very important. To do this, close your eyes and think about the emotion word you chose to describe how you're feeling now. Next, scan your body from head to toe for sensations and how the emotion is physically showing up. For example, sadness might feel like a weight or emptiness in the chest, while excitement might feel like a tingle in the spine or butterflies in the stomach!

If you like, you can use the blank body diagram below to draw how the emotion feels, using various colors, lines, and/or shapes.

3. (Optional) Ask, "Why am I feeling this way? What Automatic Thoughts am I having?"

These questions might help in realizing that you are reacting to a thought that is untrue! For example, "I was feeling sad because I assumed that person didn't like me anymore." Automatic Thoughts might also help you understand why you are feeling the way you are: "I'm so angry at my partner over the mess they made because I feel like my time isn't respected."

4. (Optional) Ask, "Am I feeling another emotion as well?"

Having two conflicting emotions can cause discomfort (for instance, relief and guilt often like to hang out together). Anger is often seen as a "second-ary emotion," meaning there is usually something (like fear or hurt) under-neath it. Taking time to be aware of *all* the emotions you are feeling can help you better make sense of your Automatic Thoughts and how you are per-ceiving a situation.

5. Respond to the emotion.

Ask yourself, "How would I like to respond to this emotion?" or, "What do I need to do, if anything, to process or alleviate this emotion? Would I like to share my happiness (or other emotion) with a friend?"

For example, you could practice some self-care by writing in a journal, or go for a walk or run. Reminding yourself that you have the choice of how to process emotions can help you to feel more in control of them. It may take individual work with a therapist to find the best processing methods for you.

If possible, it's ideal to identify and at least start to process your emo-tions before you have a conversation. This way, you're not thinking out loud, changing your mind, or processing many different emotions all while ex-pecting someone else to follow. Do you often feel like others just don't get you? This might be why! You are potentially "processing out loud," and the other person is finding it very hard to follow. If a conversation happens spontaneously, but you realize you need time to process what you're feeling, then ask! You'll learn more about this in Chapter 14 ("Setting Boundaries Skillfully").

PRACTICE MAKES ~~PERFECT~~ EASIER

Use the above steps to find and explore your emotions. Practice every day—while you're brushing your teeth, folding laundry, or commuting. Pairing this emotional check-in with an activity you already do regularly can help you remember to do it. Practicing emotional awareness daily can help build a strong emotional vocabulary and awareness, making it a lot easier for you to describe how you feel to others. In turn, you will find it a lot easier to be understood!

"I'm still not sure how I feel."

People often don't really know how they're feeling. We have a lot going on, and our feelings change constantly, so it can be tough to keep up with what's going on! In some situations, it's not necessary to know. But if a situation is causing you distress, you're going to want to get curious about your emotions. This is important, because you can only expect others to validate your reality and empathize with you if you are aware of your own reality and feelings.

If you've tried the exercises in this book and still are uncertain how you feel, you may have some blocks, such as:

* You have a lack of awareness of your emotions.
* You're too busy to identify your emotion, and now the feeling has changed.
* It's too scary.
* It's too humbling.
* You feel like you can't manage the discomfort.
* You feel you'll be stuck in the feeling if you pay too much attention to it.

Because this is a book about communication rather than self-awareness, I encourage you to go to a therapist if you are still feeling blocked. Or try some of these tips:

- Remind yourself it's okay to feel however you feel! Your reality is valid, and your feelings are normal.
- Have you had another similar experience in your past? How did you feel then? This information can help because, with hindsight, we can see emotions we felt with more objectivity. This is also a great way to remember that *feelings don't last forever*!
- Feelings can be uncomfortable and scary, and you may feel like you can't control them. That might be the case, but you *can* control how you react to the feelings. Be aware of this choice, knowing you can process and express your emotion(s) in many ways.

There are countless different reasons—personal to everyone—why blocks might come up. But they are worth exploring, because being honest about and familiar with your emotions is a very important step in being able to describe them to others and feel understood.

"I don't understand *why* I feel this way."

We sometimes react to things in ways that surprise and confuse even us! ("Why did I get so angry that my partner didn't take out the garbage? Why does it aggravate me so much when people are late? Why do I hate being stuck in traffic so much more than other people?") This is where the cognitive model, described in the Introduction (page 3), can be extremely helpful. You're not reacting to the situation; rather, *you're reacting to your thoughts about the situation*. What does the situation mean to you? What are your Automatic Thoughts? Exploring your thoughts, potentially with the help of a CBT therapist, can be crucial to understanding your reactions to various situations, normalizing those reactions, and being able to describe them to others.

"I feel many conflicting emotions."

We usually have more than one emotion at any one time, though often the strongest one takes center stage. As you build your emotional literacy and familiarity with your feelings, you may be able to identify more than one emotion. Sometimes multiple emotions are all in the same category (happiness, excitement, joy), but sometimes they're not (love, annoyance, and confusion).

When we have emotions that are conflicting, such as love and betrayal, it is *very* uncomfortable for us. Our brains try to categorize things, so having simultaneous emotions in two very distinct categories is hard. The first step to help ease this discomfort is awareness. Identify and feel all the emotions you have; write out a list if you want. Then, honor every emotion you feel. What do you need to do to process or honor each emotion? Don't try to push one away or make it smaller. Speak to someone, or to yourself, and get every emotion feeling validated! Choose as many as you want; it's okay to have many conflicting emotions!

PRACTICE MAKES ~~PERFECT~~ EASIER

To get more comfortable with having various, possibly conflicting, emotions at once, think about how you're feeling. See if the first word that comes to mind to describe how you feel has other emotions underneath it. Use the Table of Emotion Words (page 262) to help you explore other possibilities you may not have thought of. Ask yourself how feeling that first emotion might have caused or been preceded by other emotions. Revisit the cognitive model, and map out your Automatic Thoughts and reactions.

2. Communicate How You Feel

Now that you've got a handle on what's going on for you emotionally, it's time to share that with the other person. There are some important aspects to describing that will prevent or limit defensiveness in the other person and allow you to feel understood.

Switching Gears from Validating: How to Start Describing

So far, as the other person talks, you've been working on validating. But now it's your turn to talk, and you want to switch to using describing skills to talk about your own emotions. Making that shift might seem difficult. First, make sure:

1. You understand the other person's reality; and
2. They feel that you understand their reality.

As mentioned before, feeling understood will provide space for the other person to listen to you and will preemptively shut down defensiveness, because you have already shown you understand their reality (so they won't feel the urge to jump in and explain it). Once validation has been completed, you have two options: go straight into describing, or ask first. Here is what each option looks like in practice:

1. Go straight into describing: Simply start describing how you feel using "I feel _____" statements:
   - "I feel _____. . . ."

You can also use a perspective-defining lead to really emphasize that it's *your* perspective and, therefore, not a confirmed fact or an attempt to impose on the other person's reality.

- "When it comes to this, I'm feeling _____. . . ."
- "From my perspective, I feel _____. . . ."
- "The way I interpreted the situation made me feel _____"

2. Ask first. This option makes the shift from validation to describing very clear. Your aim is to ask for consent for the shift and to get the other person's buy-in to listen to what you have to say.
   - "May I tell you how I see things?"
   - "Can I let you in on my perspective?"

- "I'd love to tell you how I'm feeling about [situation]. Would that be okay with you?"

The other person's answers if they're ready to listen to you, or if you need to seek that understanding and validation elsewhere or at a later time. Your reality *is* valid, and so if you can't get validation from the conversation you're having, then you deserve to receive it from another source. (We'll discuss this more in Chapter 10.)

Delivering Bad News

When your describing includes new information for the other person, or information that you feel will most likely elicit a negative or unknown reaction, have your validation skills ready. You may have the urge to do a bit of validating beforehand, with tentative guesses as to how they might react, such as:

- "This may come as a shock to you, but . . ."

A statement like this helps them feel validated *if* their reaction is shock but can lead them to a defensive reaction if they don't feel shocked:

- "Why would you think that would shock me?"

So it's usually best to describe first, then get curious and validate the other person's reality as they describe it to you once they know the information. If you want to kick the conversation off with some positives, you can state common goals first and then launch into the describing.

- "We both want each other to be happy. I've been doing a lot of thinking and want to let you know that I've decided that it's time for me to move out and live with my partner."

Then no matter what the reaction is, validate it!

Stating Intentions before Describing

You may also feel compelled to tell the other person how you want them to interpret something before you describe your reality. (This is very similar to urges that come up when giving bad news.) And just as in bad-news situations, the preparation is probably very well-intentioned—you're trying to defuse any defensiveness before it happens. Here are a few examples:

- "Please don't take this as a personal attack, but. . . ."
- "Don't take this personally, but. . . ."
- "I don't mean to offend you, but. . . ."
- "Please don't be mad, but. . . ."

In these examples, the goal is to tell the other person how to feel (or not to feel) and how to interpret the statement you are about to make. However, we know that telling someone what to do is not a realistic, fair, or achievable goal! And, therefore, it will most likely not work.

These types of statements also impose an assumption about how the other person will react, and this may lead to them being defensive about "how they take things."

If you are feeling the urge to tell someone how to interpret your words or actions, use the skills of describing to state your intentions. Be sure to keep it positive. The examples below highlight the negative way of telling someone how *not* to feel versus the positive way of describing your intention.

Original Urge Statement	Negative Personal Goal	Positive Personal Goal
"Don't be mad/ sad, but . . ." "Don't take this personally, but . . ."	"My goal is not to hurt you."	"My goal here is to describe my perspective."
"No offense, but . . ." "Don't take this the wrong way, but . . ."	"My goal is not to confuse or offend you."	"I'm feeling worried about some of the things I want to talk to you about. My goal is to let you in on how I'm feeling."

If there is still a negative reaction to your description, despite the positive goal phrasing, validate the reaction! In Chapter 13 ("Handling Difficult Everyday Scenarios Skillfully"), we'll talk more about managing unexpected reactions.

Non-Imposing Phrasing

In describing how you feel, the phrasing you choose is key. There are ways to communicate your reality that will set you up for success. The main goal of describing is to not describe your reality as fact. When we describe our reality as fact, *we accidentally impose our own reality on the other person.* This imposition may offend anger or even confuse them. If you can be aware of how you feel and describe those feelings in a calm, non-imposing way, it's more likely that you will be heard and understood.

If you do state your reality as absolute fact, the other person may then defend their reality, which begins a cycle of defense, distracting from describing how you feel—a frustrating derailment! Below are some examples of stating your own reality as an objective fact:

- "This movie is awful."
- "You hurt me."
- "I'm the worst at . . ."
- "This is the best . . ."
- "You're wrong."

Instead, describe your reality in a non-imposing way with simple "I feel ____" statements. For example:

- "I feel frustrated."
- "I feel hurt."
- "I feel disappointed."
- "I feel happy."
- "I feel confused."

What is so great about these statements is that they describe the *only* thing that is true across all realities: how you feel! Your feelings (and the feelings of others) are always valid and real. People might argue that you "shouldn't" feel a certain way, but they can't say that you "don't" feel a certain way. (There is more later in this chapter on how to handle the response "You shouldn't feel that way.") Pointing out that feelings are the only constant across realities gets to the root of the issue and can help shut down any defensiveness or arguing about the situation. If you tell someone, "I am feeling confused (or hurt, or sad)," and they are invested in shared goals, they will want to help you, or at least be willing to hear you; you're on the same team, remember?

When "I Feel ＿＿" Statements Become Impositions

As simple as "I feel ＿＿ " statements are, they often include missteps in phrasing. People use the words "I feel" but then go on to describe their reality as fact, thereby imposing their reality. For example:

- "I feel that you're being a jerk."

This is *imposing* that the other person is being a jerk—stating it as a fact. In your reality, I'm sure they are! But in their reality, they probably aren't. So, this statement doesn't truly describe your emotion and will likely lead to them jumping in and defending themselves (and rightly so, as someone has just imposed upon their reality).

Avoiding imposing your reality is easy; avoid the word "you" in any "I feel ＿＿" statements. (You might remember a similar tip from the validation chapter, where describing starts with "I," while validating starts with "you" and is followed by an emotion word.)

For example, in the situation where you feel someone is acting like a jerk, go deeper than that: How is them being a jerk making you feel? Describe that emotion in an "I feel ＿＿" statement, where the blank is filled by a single emotion word. For example:

- "I feel very hurt."
- "I feel confused."

The following table presents examples of imposing phrasing versus non-imposing phrasing.

Imposing Describing	Non-Imposing Describing
"You're being distant." This imposes that the person *is* distant. In your reality, they seem distant, but in their reality, they might not be distant. If they don't think they are being distant, they will jump to defend: "No, I'm not." The conversation will turn into an argument over whether they're distant or not, completely ignoring your hurt and curiosity about why they seem different.	"I'm feeling like things are off lately, and I'm getting worried." You could also take it a step further and invite them, using open-ended questions, to describe their reality (and be ready to validate). "I was wondering if you could help me by telling me what's been going on for you lately?"
"You're angry." "I feel like you're angry." This uses the word "you" to label the other person.	How do you *feel* seeming angry? "I'm feeling hurt and frustrated right now." "I feel confused."
"Do you even like me?" Instead of being genuinely curious, you're imposing your own reality with a leading, closed-ended, yes/no question and assuming they don't like you. This could also be seen as provoking someone else, or stirring the pot to further fan the flames of an argument.	"How do you feel about our relationship?" This is an open-ended question (that can't be answered with a yes/no) and doesn't lead the other person or impose your reality on them.
"This food sucks." You're making a statement as if it's fact when it is your opinion.	"I'm not enjoying this food." "I feel disappointed by this meal." You're clearly stating what's going on in your reality.

Imposing Describing	Non-Imposing Describing
"You never do the dishes." This presents your reality as fact.	*"To me, it feels like I'm always the one doing the dishes, which is really stressful."* Avoiding the word "you" and instead using "I" statements, plus a perspective-defining lead, points out it's your reality, not a fact, and is therefore not imposing.
"I feel you don't understand." Although this starts with "I feel," the word "you" comes right after and imposes your reality (they don't understand) onto the other person.	Try asking them what they're thinking, rather than assuming they're confused. *"I'm wondering how you think or feel the situation went. Do you mind describing it to me from your perspective?"* Validate what they say (even if it's "wrong" to you), then describe your reality again. *"Oh, so you're feeling that the reason I was crying earlier was because of _____. I can see how that might look from the outside. I was crying because of _____."*
"I feel like you're mad at me." We have a good start with "I feel," but then the "like you" imposes that they're mad, which they might not be.	Ask an open-ended question, letting them describe for themselves how they're feeling: *"How are you feeling toward me right now?"* Or be tentative, and give the chance for correction: *"I'm getting the sense you're mad at me. Is that right?"* Or ask yourself, how does them seeming mad at you make you feel? *"I'm feeling uneasy/guilty/mad about this situation."*

The adjusted phrases in the right-hand column describe your emotions, while inviting your conversation partner to help. They avoid accusations or statements of fact (imposing your reality).

PRACTICE MAKES ~~PERFECT~~ EASIER

Try the "I feel ____" statements with various people in your life. How do they react? How does their reaction make you feel? Are they validating? Or do they start talking about themselves? Being aware of what it's like on the receiving end can really help you become both a better validator and a better describer.

Accusatory Emotion Words

Emotions can be tough to describe, and many words that describe emotions can also come across as accusatory, which can result in defensiveness. For example, saying, "I felt abandoned when I didn't get to see you last weekend," or, "I feel judged by that comment," is more likely to be interpreted as an accusation. To the receiver, these statements sound like "You abandoned me," and "You're judging me." Here are some other common verbs/adjectives that can sound accusatory.

Abandon(ed)	Brush(ed) Off	Judge(d)	Patronize(d)
Accuse(d)	Condemn(ed)	Misinterpret(ed)	Pressure(d)
Antagonize(d)	Condescend(ed)	Neglect(ed)	Resent(ed)
Attack(ed)	Dismiss(ed)	Offend(ed)	Rush(ed)
Belittle(d)	Insult(ed)	Oppress(ed)	Threaten(ed)

Using these words might go well, and that's great! This is a bit of a gray area, but if you are trying to set up a successful conversation with someone who is prone to being defensive, it might be in your best interest to look for other words to describe your reality. Instead of using one of the words listed, ask yourself how that action or word (for example, being abandoned or judged) made you feel. Look for the emotion underneath. Here are some examples of how to do it:

Accusatory Words	Non-Accusatory Words
"I felt abandoned when I didn't get to see you last weekend."	*"I feel lonely and sad because I didn't get to see you last weekend."*
"I feel judged by that comment."	*"I feel really hurt because, to me, that comment makes me feel like I'm not good enough."*

Describing How You Think Versus How You Feel

Sometimes it can be tempting, or necessary, to describe your thoughts about a situation rather than your feelings. For instance, in logical decision-making, such as when choosing a brand of facial tissue at the store, or when collaborating with coworkers on a project, heavy emotion words might not be necessary or helpful. When someone is in "thought mode," they might use words such as:

- agree/disagree
- believe
- doubt
- imagine
- know
- remember/forget
- suspect
- think
- understand

As helpful as describing our thoughts can be, sometimes it's also tempting to stay in a more logical, thought-oriented mindset because the emotions and feelings can be scary, unfamiliar, or uncomfortable. Depending on the situation, you might want to know what emotions are involved. If that's the case, you can ask, "How do you *feel* about this situation?" Refer to the Table of Emotion Words (page 262) and the section on how to find your emotions, earlier in this chapter, if you (or the other person) need help.

Being Concise Versus Telling the Entire Story

Notice how most of the examples in this chapter don't go into describing *why* you feel a certain way. They simply describe the emotion and show that there doesn't need to be justification, since the emotion is valid and real for you.

Whether you want to go into more detail about *why* you feel the way you do will be up to you and should be decided based upon who you're talking to. Depending on the other person, it might be in your best interests to keep your describing concise, without reasons as to why you feel the way you do. Why? Because reasons can be ammunition for an argument. Giving reasons as to why you feel the way you do is like throwing a really easy ball in the air so the other person can knock it right back at you and tell you why your reasoning is "wrong." Some argumentative or difficult people might even bait you into giving them reasons so that they can argue each one and try to talk you out of how you feel.

On the flip side, the other person might have an honest intention to know your reality better by understanding the situation and the Automatic Thoughts that caused your reaction. Use your best judgment, depending on the person and your interactions with them in the past. You can either explain (using more describing skills), or you can say, "That is simply how I feel."

You may feel you need to describe more than just how you're feeling—you might want to explain a situation you saw unfold or your entire experience of an event. This is a valid need, and storytelling is awesome! This is where you make a judgment call about what is most important for the conversation. What is your personal goal? If moving on to solutions is most important, then being concise is the best option. If you really need the other person to understand your perspective on an entire situation, then describe the whole thing! If you are unsure, you can first test the waters with a non-imposing emotional description, such as with an "I feel ____" statement. If the other person is open, you can then share more about what is happening with you. If, on the other hand, you think the conversation might escalate or get caught up in defense of realities, err on the side of being as concise as possible while still meeting your personal goal for the conversation. When doing this, it's still very important to keep in mind that *you are describing* your *reality only.*

- "I was feeling really hurt by [the situation]. I was left feeling confused, and to me it seemed like [description of events]."

In this example, a perspective-defining lead like "to me, it seemed" can help show that you are describing your reality, or your perspective of events, not a factual reality that is clear to everyone. Another example:

- "From my perspective, you seemed really angry with me, and I was hurt by that because my intention was not to make you angry."

You can see how this is different than "You were really angry," which would be imposing that as fact onto their reality. They might have *seemed* angry to you, but instead they were flustered, confused, hurt, or another emotion. So, it's important to describe *your interpretation*, and to phrase it as such.

At other times, you might just want to vent, describing events to a friend or therapist who you know is there to listen:

- "Then I spilled my coffee on my new pants, and I had to still go to the meeting, and it was really uncomfortable and embarrassing. I felt like I wanted to cry halfway through the meeting, but I made it through and am feeling a lot better. But now I am just mentally exhausted!"

Or:

- "I finished my last test. Now it's summer break, and I am feeling super relieved and happy!"

If the Other Person Doesn't Validate You

Now that you've described how you feel, you might find that it has landed very well and the other person understands and validates you. However, sometimes the other person in a conversation may not be in a place to provide validation, or they may not know how. Either way, your reality is *still valid*, and you will likely want to seek that validation elsewhere. (See Chapter 10 ("Practice Self-Care") for more about how to do this.) In learning to accept another person's validation limitations, you might also want to get curious about why they're *not* able to validate your experience. Consider what blocks came up for them. Understanding their reality can be helpful to you both.

If you are feeling up for it, you can teach people how to validate. Share some of the tips from this book, or say to them, "What I need from you right now is to reflect back how I'm feeling so I can feel understood by you. Would you be willing to try that?"

If the Other Person Invalidates You

"Don't be mad."

"Don't feel sad."

"Don't get stressed."

"You shouldn't feel annoyed by that."

These types of comments can really make our blood boil! Not only is the other person not validating you, they're actually *invalidating* you.

Although we've already established that the only thing consistent across realities is how you feel, some might still argue you *shouldn't* feel a certain way. Being told how to feel can be extremely frustrating, because someone is imposing their reality onto you. As we learned way back in Chapter 1, changing someone's feelings is not a realistic goal, but that doesn't mean people won't try.

Ironically, when someone is trying to tell you how to feel, the first thing for you to do to defuse the situation is to *validate them*. They're most likely feeling shocked, confused, or guilty that you feel the way you do, so try:

- "You seem shocked that I'm angry about this."
- "The fact that I'm feeling jealous seems to be confusing for you."
- "It seems that you feel really bad and guilty that I was hurt."

Or try imagining that when they're saying, "You shouldn't feel ____," what they're really saying is, "It wasn't my intention to make you feel ____." You can then respond to that using validation:

- "It seems like it wasn't your intention to make me angry, so you're shocked about my reaction."
- "The fact that I'm feeling jealous seems to be confusing for you because you wouldn't feel jealous if the situation were reversed."
- "It seems that you feel really bad that I was hurt. I'm wondering about why you feel that way; is it because you didn't mean to hurt me?"

Then you can gently redirect the conversation back to describing with the "I feel ____" statements.

- "You seem shocked that I'm angry about this, perhaps because it wasn't your intention to make me angry. But I do feel angry."
- "The fact that I'm feeling jealous seems to be confusing for you, maybe because you wouldn't feel jealous if the situation were reversed. I am feeling really jealous right now though."
- "It seems that you feel bad that I was hurt, maybe because you care about me and never want to hurt me. In any case, I did feel quite hurt."

Changing the Past Culture of Invalidation

Now that you're learning new techniques for communicating, it might seem difficult to change old cycles. You might know how to validate, but your conversation partner might not. Using these techniques can be a great way to start the change. Stay calm, validate, and provide positive reinforcement. Give them a copy of this book, or a free lesson! Be patient with yourself and the other person. Change takes time. Celebrate any success, not matter how small or large, with credit and/or positive reinforcement (both described in detail later in the book)!

THINGS TO CONSIDER WHEN YOU'RE DESCRIBING

"I'm Afraid of How the Other Person Will React"

Sometimes we don't know how a conversation will go or how the other person will react, and that makes us scared or hesitant to describe our reality. That unknown can be scary! It can be so scary that you keep your reality to yourself. Doing this might be warranted in some situations, as the other person may not be ready to accept your reality. However, keeping your reality to yourself more than you need to can also lead to resentment, loneliness, and other negative consequences. If you're feeling scared to share your reality, try asking yourself the following questions:

- Would it be beneficial to share my reality and my emotions?
- What might happen if I described my reality? How would I feel?
- What might happen if I din't describe my reality? How would I feel?
- What are you scared of (the other person's reaction, hurting them, being misunderstood)?
- What's the worst that could happen? How could you cope with that?
- Have similar situations happened in the past, and if so, how did you cope with those?
- What are your common goals for this relationship?
- What are your personal goals for this conversation?

If you want to describe but are still feeling scared, practice the conversation with someone else you trust to get a different perspective on your verbal and nonverbal communication. This can also help raise your comfort level with your own abilities to cope with the conversation and feel emotionally and mentally prepared.

If you have been unintentionally hurt by someone, it can also be difficult expressing that you are hurt—because you know that their intention was not to hurt you and that telling them you're hurt will most likely cause them discomfort. But it's okay! We are all uncomfortable at times, and you can let them know how you're feeling and validate their intention and also their discomfort about you feeling hurt. By doing this, you start building a relationship culture where it's not the end of the world if someone is hurt or uncomfortable. You can have confidence in your skills to understand each other, find solutions, and move on!

More about Tone

As we discussed in the previous chapter, tone is extremely important when it comes to communication. If you have issues with people misinterpreting you (and you know you're speaking very clearly), it may be your tone. To explore this further, ask another person to help. Have a discussion with a trusted friend who can let you know when your tone doesn't match the words you are saying. Or if you're on the receiving end of a tone that feels uncomfortable or offends you, ask for clarification and then practice validation. For example:

- "I heard you say that you're okay with me going out with my friends tonight while you stay home, but I'm getting the sense that you're not okay with it. Do you mind telling me a bit more about how you're feeling?"

Saying "I'm Fine!"

As a therapist, and a human, I run into this phrase often—a disingenuous "I'm fine," where the tone does not match the words, and it's obvious that the person saying it is not fine at all. "I'm fine!" seems to have been accepted by many as a phrase to use when you need something. That something might be time, space, reassurance, solutions, help, or a myriad of other things.

There is absolutely nothing wrong with needing any of those things! However, there *is* something wrong with falsely advertising how you feel and making the other person guess your needs. Saying you're fine when you're not creates a relationship culture of confusion, makes the other person guess, and *sets them up to fail*. It also makes it okay for the other person to use that phrase in the future, further increasing the confusion and lack of communication of needs in the relationship. (Can you tell how much I am not fine with the response "I'm fine"?)

As an antidote, next time someone says, "I'm fine," try these responses:

* "I'm getting the sense that's not the case, but I may be wrong. Either way, I'm here if you need to talk."
* "I'm happy to give you some time and space if you need to sort something out."
* "I am wondering if I missed something; can you please explain to me what your perspective was on what just happened?"
* "I hear you say you're feeling fine about this situation, but I'm curious—what else are you feeling?"

Be ready to follow these questions with validation. Someone's urge to say "I'm fine" might come up because they are ashamed of how they feel, or because they're scared that expressing how they feel might not go over well or that they might not get their needs met. Either way, they're having an urge to keep things inside. Being an open recipient for their reality description can help stop "I'm fine" behavior.

And if saying "I'm fine" is something that *you* tend to do in conversations, the next time *you* feel the urge to say it, try one of these phrases instead:

* "I need some time to process how I'm feeling before I tell you."
* "I'm frustrated because I don't feel understood, so I need some time to calm down before we talk about this."
* "I'm not okay, but I'm not ready to talk about it."

- "I appreciate you asking, but I honestly don't know how I'm feeling right now."
- "I'm worried about expressing how I feel about the situation."

With these phrases, you are describing what's going on for you and asking for what you need. These alternatives help create a relationship culture where it's okay for the other person to use these alternate phrases as well, leading to more understanding and communication.

When to Describe *Before* You Validate

I ordered the skills of communication to highlight the importance of validation, as it is the part that usually comes least naturally and is a great stand-alone skill to default to. However, in some rare circumstances, you'll need to switch the order of validating and describing. This typically comes into play when you have new information to share. For example, when:

- Breaking up with someone
- Giving someone good news
- Leaving a job
- Firing someone
- Telling someone you've decided to move out

The other skills can then work in the same order presented.

When to Omit Describing

Depending on your goals, you may want to leave out the describing step altogether. Your reality is every bit as valid as anyone else's; however, sometimes describing can get in the way of reaching the goals for a conversation. For example, if you are comforting a friend, student, or child who is in a distressing situation, the goal is to listen and validate them, not to describe how you're feeling. Or when someone is extremely defensive, but you still need to work with them to find solutions, then skipping or limiting the describing you do can head off more defensiveness, so you can get to the next step—solution finding—more quickly and efficiently. Finally, if you are in a position of power (a parent, boss, or teacher, for instance), consider shortening or leaving out the describing step, as the power dynamic is a big factor and you might accidentally steamroll the other person.

Remember, in these situations, your reality is still valid! Make sure you can find that validation elsewhere so you are able to practice self-care. (You'll learn more about this in Chapter 10.)

Alternating between Describing and Validating

Often conversations will bounce back and forth between validation and describing before you're able to move to the next step of finding solutions. Be patient. As mentioned before, taking in and accepting someone else's reality can be very difficult, so your conversation partner may need some time to process your reality. Likewise, you may need time to fully understand their reality. Taking the time to fully understand each other sets the foundation for success with finding solutions.

Who Goes First?

When I started counseling couples, I would often ask myself, "Who gets to describe their reality first?" I wondered if my choosing one person to go first would lead to assumptions about that person's reality being *more* valid than the other's. Then I realized: *someone has to go first*. I wish we could both describe and validate each other's reality at the same time, but that's just not possible. People need to take turns, and this requires awareness and patience. Oftentimes it's best to let the person who is in the most distress go first, as they are the person most in need of validation. If you can't decide, you can always let the other person go first, and know that you will get your turn later.

When someone else is describing, be aware of any urges you may have to jump in. If this happens, take a breath, listen, and remember that you'll get your turn eventually, whether it's in this conversation or later, as a part of your self-care plan. Remember how important validation is to create the space for you to describe your own reality later.

BOTTOM LINE

Describing your reality and having it validated is extremely important because your reality is valid! To receive this validation, you can set yourself up for success by using language that doesn't impose your reality on someone else. Being aware of your emotions and describing them using "I feel" statements is a simple and effective way to describe your reality. Modeling this type of behavior can have a positive impact on communication.

Chapter 8

FIND SOLUTIONS

10 SKILLS OF COMMUNICATION

1. Set Personal Goals
2. Choose a Time, Place, and Platform
3. Calm Down (Enough)
4. Remember to Listen
5. State Common Goals
6. Validate
7. Describe
8. **Find Solutions**
9. Offer Positive Reinforcement
10. Practice Self-Care

INTRODUCTION

Have you ever felt like you're having the same argument again and again? This is most likely because you have never gotten to the solution-finding part of the conversation. The seven communication skills you've learned so far have laid a strong foundation to help with the next skill, which is to find solutions. Finding solutions is often an integral part of achieving personal conversation goals, especially if we have the intent to motivate some change in the other person! In this chapter, I explain how to know if solution-finding is needed, and if it is, how to find solutions and address common blocks to compromising.

FINDING SOLUTIONS: WHY IT'S IMPORTANT

The step of finding solutions often gets skipped when two conversation partners get stuck in defending their realities, and then get too tired to finish the conversation. Or maybe you got to the solution-finding step, and you and your conversation partner agreed, "Okay, this will change," but because you hadn't come up with a specific solution, no change happened. If you aren't *specific* about new solutions to try, and changes to make to reach those solutions, you'll automatically revert back to the old way of doing things. The same argument happens again and again; nothing changes, there is no new outcome. Finding solutions is key to breaking these cycles.

However, there are some situations where finding solutions is not necessary. To determine whether you need a solution for your particular scenario, ask yourself, "Is there change needed?" or, "Is there a problem that needs solving?"

For example, solution-finding is not needed when:

- hearing about someone's day or telling them about yours
- comforting a friend or family member
- describing your frustration to someone else

It is needed if:

- you feel as though your colleague is not pulling their weight in a group project
- a teenager in your family keeps sleeping in and missing the bus
- you feel like your partner keeps criticizing you
- your friend's car broke down

FINDING SOLUTIONS: HOW TO DO IT

As I said in the introduction to this chapter, the communication skills you've learned thus far can be very useful in setting up solution-finding.

Have your personal goals in mind; choose a good time, place, and platform; calm down (enough); remember to listen; and state common goals. It can also be helpful to do some validating, to ensure you understand the other person. If they are open to it, describing is also helpful because it creates understanding on both sides. As stated in "Behavioral Urges That Block Validation" (page 73), it can be tough not to jump to finding solutions right away. However, finding solutions without first knowing each other's realities is very difficult because the needs of each person are not yet clear and understood by everyone in the conversation. When you feel that both of you have validated and described as much as is needed, move on to the skills for finding solutions. Here's a step-by-step list for how to do it:

1. Restate common goals

State your common goals again. This will remind you both of the reason you're having the conversation and align you as a team that's setting out to solve the issue together.

2. State both sets of needs

Now that you each understand the other's reality, you should have a good idea about what each person's needs are. State both sets of needs. They may be conflicting. If so, note that difference:

- "So, you have the need to relax on the weekend, whereas I have the need to get things done so that I feel prepared for the week."
- "We each seem to have different views on how to spend the weekends. You like to relax, and I like to be involved in activities."

3. Propose compromises

Before the conversation (if possible), it's helpful to consider potential compromises to get the ball rolling on solutions. Then, when you get to this stage, you can suggest a solution that bridges the needs of both people. Be specific—who is doing what, how, and when?

- "We could try doing the chores on Friday after work and then relaxing for the rest of the weekend."
- "I can do my chores on Saturday, you can do your activities on Saturday, and then we can hang out together on Sundays."

Notice the language here uses the word "we" or uses both "you" and "I." This shows teamwork and compromise; the actions don't rest solely on one person.

4. Ask for input

Ask for input in the form of open-ended questions (which you learned about in Chapter 6):

- "What do you think of that plan?"
- "How does that solution sit with you?"
- "What else do you think we could try?"

Use this process to brainstorm multiple solutions. Consider making a list to keep track of them all.

5. Agree to try something new

Choose one of the solutions to try. Again, be as specific as possible, and iron out all the details. Who does what? How? When? Put your heads together, and consider if there will be any blocks to using the new solution; if so, how can you overcome those? Thinking through possible problems in the solution can really set you up for success.

- "So, we'll try doing chores on Friday evening. If even one of us is too tired, we'll move them to Saturday morning instead."

Try out the new solutions for a predetermined time. Don't get too attached to any one solution. Remembering your common goals, as well as seeing what's worked and what hasn't, can be helpful in remaining open to compromise. Nothing is written in stone, and the team is in charge!

6. Set a date to check in

After the predetermined trial period, check in about how the solution is working. Knowing you have a set date to check in with each other minimizes resistance to trying new solutions. Being open also models the behavior you'd like to see in the other person.

- "Let's experiment. We can try this for this month and then check in about how it's going."

At the check-in, use the communication skills you've learned. For example, your personal goal for the check-in could be to understand the other person's experience with the solution. You can then make sure you understand (and show you understand) through validation, and describe your own experience with the solution. Then, if needed, try a different solution.

Blocks to Finding Solutions

The six steps listed above should give you a good framework for finding solutions. However, in real life, things don't always go according to plan! Here are a few situations I see in which finding solutions can be a bit messier.

The Other Person Won't Compromise

If you've suggested solutions but the other person isn't willing to budge, reassess your goals and your proposed solution. Are you asking way too much? Are any of the expectations unreasonable? If you're not sure, consider asking a neutral third party to weigh in to get a different perspective.

Next, show your teammate that you're willing to meet them halfway, or more than halfway. Restate the different realities you both have and show how your proposed compromise fits somewhere in the middle of both sets of wants/needs. This is modeling the behavior you want to see in return.

If the other person has the goal of imposing their reality on you, or having you abandon your reality to agree with theirs (neither of which are realistic goals), they might also not be willing or able to come up with compromises. If they are still seeking their way 100 percent, you might need to decide whether to accept their request for now, look for solutions elsewhere, or end the relationship. (If you need to end the relationship, you'll find support in Chapter 15 ("Ending Relationships Skillfully").)

"I Care More That They Are Happy"

You're nice, so the urge to put your own needs aside and use the solution that the other person prefers feels easier. Maybe you have no emotional investment in this particular situation, so it's really not a big deal to agree with the other person's solution. Keeping your needs to yourself seems harmless! Still, it's really helpful for you (and the other person) to describe your reality and your ideal scenario.

I work with clients who are on the receiving end of an "overcompromiser," and I've seen that they can become very frustrated; they don't know if there is resentment building, and they feel like the other person is just agreeing with everything they say. To them, it feels really one-sided, which, despite getting their needs met, is a very uncomfortable place to be! For solution-finding to be successful, both parties need to know where the edges are, so you can reach the middle ground (aka compromise land). If you are too willing to overcompromise, the other person might even get too used to "getting their way" and be less willing to compromise in future situations where you *do* want some compromise. Being aware of your ideal situation, being able to communicate it, and then coming up with compromises is a great way to create a stable relationship culture.

State your ideal situation, but then mention you are more than happy to be closer to their ideal situation (if that's indeed true), and say why. This way, both of you will feel you are invested in the outcome, understand the other person, are not building unspoken resentments, and feel confident in the ability to find middle ground in future situations.

Binary Solutions

Sometimes there is no room for compromise. To find middle ground with these situations, compromise in *other* areas of the relationship instead. Most of the time, even small compromises can be made and tried.

For example, the decision to go on a trip has a binary solution: you go, or you don't go. However, there can be compromises in other areas, such as openness to future trips, a shorter duration for the trip, where you will stay, and so on. Compromise in other areas will depend on the reasons to go/not go on the trip. For example, if it's a financial concern, limited options for taking time off work, or missing your time with friends, these areas could be modified.

> **PRACTICE MAKES ~~PERFECT~~ EASIER**

Think about a problem you've seen two characters on a TV show have or that you've read about two people having in a book or article. What are both of their realities? What are each of their ideal outcomes? Can you think of some compromises or solutions they could try? Bring in someone else to help you brainstorm—you might find they come up with ideas that are different from your own.

BOTTOM LINE

Finding solutions together can be a very productive part of communication, if done effectively. Solutions will help create new ways of handling your interactions and needs, so you don't get caught up in the same cycle. Being willing to compromise, get creative, and try new solutions as a team can also build a shared history of success!

Chapter 9

OFFER POSITIVE REINFORCEMENT

10 SKILLS OF COMMUNICATION

1. Set Personal Goals
2. Choose a Time, Place, and Platform
3. Calm Down (Enough)
4. Remember to Listen
5. State Common Goals
6. Validate
7. Describe
8. Find Solutions
9. **Offer Positive Reinforcement**
10. Practice Self-Care

INTRODUCTION

How do you end a conversation once you've reached your goals? In the previous chapters, you learned skills for how to prepare for, start, and have a conversation, so now you are ready to learn how to wrap things up! Positive reinforcement[6] is a great way to end conversations naturally and on a positive note. It is also one of my favorite tools because it can be used as a stand-alone skill that helps create more positive, understanding relationships and allows us to practice expressing our reality in a positive way. This chapter will explain why positive reinforcement is important, how it can be used to end conversations, how it's different from complimenting someone, and more!

POSITIVE REINFORCEMENT: WHY IT'S IMPORTANT

The skill of positive reinforcement clearly communicates what someone is doing well. It directly rewards behavior we *like*, making it more likely that we'll see that behavior again. We often point out in others (and in ourselves) behaviors we don't like because that's what needs changing—and there's nothing wrong with that (if done respectfully)! However, *only* pointing out things you don't like can lead to a lack of balance between negative and positive statements, which creates a negative dynamic in the relationship. Bringing in more positive reinforcement is a simple way to reset that balance.

If you are looking to wrap up and finish an intense or emotionally charged conversation, positive reinforcement is a great tool to change perspectives and to end things on a positive note.

Not only is positive reinforcement a helpful skill to be used in conversations, it's also a great stand-alone tool. For example, if your partner took out the garbage and you didn't say anything, they might take out the garbage again, or they might not. But if you gave them a big hug afterward, and said, "Thank you so much for taking out the garbage; I really appreciate it," or made them dinner and told them it was because of their small gesture, they'd probably be extremely inclined to take the garbage out again in the future!

POSITIVE REINFORCEMENT: HOW TO DO IT

First, find a *behavior* that you like and want to see again. What has someone done that you really appreciated?

- Listened to you
- Respected your boundaries

- Done something nice for you
- Said something nice to you
- Helped you with something
- Validated you

Once you have a behavior in mind, there are many options to provide positive reinforcement.

1. Offer simple gratitude, thanks, and appreciation.

- "Thank you for making me dinner; I really appreciate it."
- "Thank you for being so patient and listening to my perspective."
- "I am really grateful that you are working so hard in couples therapy."

(Notice how these are more specific than only saying "Thank you" or "I appreciate that.")

2. Describe the positive effects on your reality.

- "It helped me get so much work done when you took care of the kids last night."
- "From my perspective, our mornings run so much smoother when you get out of bed on time."

(Notice how these are more specific than "That helped me so much" or "My morning was so much better today.")

3. Describe your positive emotions.

- "I feel so happy when you remember to save me some coffee in the morning."
- "When you remember to be on time, I feel really cared for and loved."

(Notice these aren't just "I feel _____" statements but are pointing out that the other person's behavior is the reason for the positive feeling.)

4. Describe how the behavior helps your common goals.

- "I love when you take the time to do your share of the chores, because it means we are both happier in our home and we can spend more time together."
- "When we listen to each other and you validate my reality, it helps us have really peaceful communication where we can explore solutions together."

(You're pointing out specific things they did well to help achieve the common goals you have.)

Positive Reinforcement to End Conversations

Positive reinforcement to end a conversation can be done using any of the above techniques and rewards what the other person did well during the conversation. Even if there were aspects of the conversation that didn't go well, thanking someone for listening to your perspective, not interrupting, or being vulnerable in describing their feelings can be extremely powerful and ends things on a positive note.

- "Thank you for being patient and listening to my perspective."
- "I appreciate your effort to understand how I'm feeling by reflecting what I am feeling."
- "I feel so relieved that we were able to calmly discuss solutions and you helped brainstorm some compromises."
- Give a hug to express appreciation.

Compliments Versus Positive Reinforcement

I have seen clients confuse positive reinforcement and compliments—they are similar in some ways. However, complimenting is about praising *attributes, abilities,* or *talents,* like how someone looks, sings, cooks, etc. Positive reinforcement is about praising *chosen behavior that affects you both in a positive way.* This is one reason why it's important to be specific (positive reinforcement, as in, "Great work cleaning the living room; I really appreciate it, and now we have more time to spend together!") versus being general (a compliment, as in, "You're such a tidy person.").

Negative Behavior (An Excuse to Punish?)

You may be wondering what to do with behavior you *don't* want to see and if certain forms of punishment may be necessary to deter the behavior. In conversations, punishment typically takes the form of negative words or actions—complaining, yelling, and criticizing are some examples—in the hopes that the other person will change their behavior so they don't suffer the consequences. These can sometimes be effective in stopping behavior but are usually damaging to the relationship in the process.

If there are negative behaviors that need to stop, take a breath, then ask yourself if there's a way to ignore the negative behavior and instead positively reinforce the desired behavior.

For example, your child wants a cookie, and you've said no. They start whining. Instead of yelling at them to stop whining, can you ignore them until they eventually stop? Don't look at them or engage with their behavior in any way. Then, once they stop whining, let them know you appreciate that they stopped, give them a hug, and tell them they can have a cookie after dinner/tomorrow/whenever the next time for a treat is.

If positive reinforcement doesn't fit the scenario, but you still want to maintain the relationship without using punishment, try boundary-setting instead (see Chapter 14).

Accidentally Reinforcing Negative Behaviors

Now that you're aware of behaviors you like, it might be time to think about accidental positive reinforcement. Is there something your family member, colleague, partner, or friend keeps doing again and again, despite you asking them not to? You might be unaware of your own role in keeping this behavior going.

For example, your child has a tantrum, and you resist. But they persist, and eventually you finally give in. By giving in to the yelling, you've just taught them if they yell enough, they'll eventually get what they want. Or you ask your partner to take the garbage out, and they don't do it right away, so you just do it. You've just taught them that if they don't do their chores, someone else will do them eventually. I have firsthand experience with this: I've had to leave dishes unwashed longer than I like because I don't want my partner to assume that I'll end up doing them. We've come to an agreement that he will clean them up at least once per week, and we did this using the boundary-setting techniques presented later in this book.

One piece of positive reinforcement we often overlook as a "reward" is our attention. Needs for attention may be more obvious in children and animals, but attention can also be a reward for many different people. Once you are aware of this, treat your attention (positive or negative) as currency. Notice any attention-seeking behaviors. If you think this is happening, and the behavior is not presenting an immediate danger, do your best to ignore it, because punishment or attention of *any* kind will give the other person what they want and therefore unintentionally reinforce the behavior. Remain neutral and let them get tired of trying for attention. Then reward the behavior you do like.

"This Feels Like Animal Training"

If you're a pet owner, and using positive reinforcement sounds like animal training, it's because the learning principles are the same. In my past career as an aquarium biologist, I trained many exotic animals: sharks, stingrays, even a sea turtle! Can you think of a way to punish a shark? It's impossible (without resorting to inhumane methods). Without getting into too much detail, the only way to train animals like sharks is to use a rewards-only system—in other words, positive reinforcement!

Using only positive reinforcement, and no punishment, has also been found to be a beneficial way to train dogs. With dogs, you can ignore bad behavior (basically, giving bad behavior no reinforcement) and then reinforce good behavior with food and praise and attention. This leaves the relationship between dog and trainer far more intact than it would if you were constantly punishing them! The same can be said for your personal relationships.

If practicing what feels like animal training feels uncomfortable to you, feel free to rename positive reinforcement to a term that works for you—acknowledgment, praise, or rewards. Consider, too, that it's *your* behavior that's changing first. Also, remember that you are not using any of these techniques to avoid validating the other person's reality or trying to impose your reality on them. It's all about keeping interactions as productive as possible for the good of the relationship.

PRACTICE MAKES ~~PERFECT~~ EASIER

Challenge yourself to use positive reinforcement with someone in your life once today. Then tomorrow, do it twice; the next day, three times; then four. . . . Start noticing the different scenarios where this can be applied. You may see how often good behavior has gone unrewarded and unacknowledged!

If positive reinforcement seems awkward at first, that is completely normal! It's a potential sign you need to do it more often. Enjoy this great opportunity to see some amazing changes in your relationships!

THE CREDIT EXERCISE:
POSITIVE REINFORCEMENT FOR *YOU*

I developed the Credit Exercise to help build self-esteem and practice positive reinforcement. If you are finding it difficult to start with positive reinforcement for others, this is how you can try it on yourself first!

I created the Credit Exercise after being inspired by gratitude practices. With gratitude, instead of focusing on what we don't have or what we want to change, we draw attention to what we are grateful for and what we do have.

Hearing about, and seeing, the effects of gratitude, I decided to take it to an individual level. Clients come to me with the things they don't like about themselves, or the things they want to change or need help with. This is great to focus their goals and shows a high level of self-awareness. However, sometimes this perspective is not balanced with thoughts of how far they've come, their strengths, and the specific things they've done well.

To remedy this, I prescribe taking between one and five minutes at the end of the day to mentally give yourself credit for two things you did well that day. It can be literally anything! Some examples are going to therapy, remembering to do breathing exercises, initiating a difficult conversation,

or even taking a shower. Nothing is too big or small. After a while, try three things, then four, or even five!

Again, the purpose of this exercise is not to ignore the work that still needs to be done; it's to provide *balance* between future and past achievements. This exercise works wonders to help build self-esteem as well!

With the Credit Exercise, it's important to remember that your baseline will change. For clients who are feeling depressed, it's an achievement to take a shower and brush their teeth. When they are feeling better, those things are easier, so they give themselves credit for going to work or trying a new sport. Realizing that everyone's baseline changes, credit earned on different days will be different, and that's okay! Celebrate the small and large successes. Life can be hard, so any success deserves credit. We all deserve to celebrate our successes and give attention to the things we *are* doing well.

A more advanced version of the Credit Exercise is to think about the things you are working on, such as personal goals, academic goals, career goals, or relationship goals. Pair the Credit Exercise with future-focused thinking to help balance your thoughts; remind yourself of how far you've already come in those goal areas, rather than ruminating on how far you still need to go, and you'll feel more at peace.

BOTTOM LINE

Point out and praise behaviors you like. Use rewards to positively reinforce specific behaviors you want to see again. This creates positivity and balance within the relationship without accidentally reinforcing unproductive behavior.

Chapter 10

PRACTICE SELF-CARE

10 SKILLS OF COMMUNICATION

1. Set Personal Goals
2. Choose a Time, Place, and Platform
3. Calm Down (Enough)
4. Remember to Listen
5. State Common Goals
6. Validate
7. Describe
8. Find Solutions
9. Offer Positive Reinforcement
10. **Practice Self-Care**

INTRODUCTION

Self-care is such a buzzword these days, but what exactly is it? This chapter explores different types of self-care and how they fit into difficult conversations and communication scenarios.

SELF-CARE: WHY IT'S IMPORTANT

Taking care of yourself after a difficult or emotionally intense conversation is important to mentally process, physically regulate, emotionally regulate, and come to terms with new information. As I define it with my clients, self-care is different from simply relaxing or resting our physical body. Relaxing is necessary, but self-care is different in that it includes a mental component.

Self-care focuses on your mind, whether that means allowing time to deliberately process thoughts during a walk or watching TV to give your mind a rest from your thought patterns. Self-care can take many forms and is very personal. Taking the time to find activities that give your mind what it needs can help with mood, emotional regulation, and even quality of sleep!

SELF-CARE: HOW TO DO IT

There are so many ways to practice self-care, I've divided them into different categories: emotional, logistical, physical, and spiritual.

Emotional Self-Care

Emotional self-care is very important. Having this type of self-care allows us to be aware of our emotions, gives us time to process them, and helps us feel understood. Below are three ways to focus self-care on emotions.

1. Seek Validation

This is potentially the most important step! Sometimes the other person does not have the capacity or skills to validate or understand you, or maybe the situation just didn't call for you to describe your reality. If you did not feel heard, understood, or validated by another person in a conversation, it's important you get your reality validated elsewhere, because *your reality is valid!* To do this, you can:

1. Speak with a therapist, friend, or family member who will validate your reality.
2. Journal or speak to yourself out loud to validate your own reality.
3. Listen to music, read poems, or focus on a piece of art that you relate to and that describes a similar experience to the one you're having.

The Difference between Seeking Validation and Complaining

Getting validation is feeling understood and being able to move on. Complaining is invalidating another person's reality and trying to prove their reality wrong, which, as we've learned, is a fruitless effort. (In some cases, it's simple gossip.) Not only will complaining not lead to a resolution, but it is also hard on the person who hears it.

When you are seeking validation from a third party, remain aware that your goal is not to prove the other person's reality wrong, invalidate their reality, or convince the third party to agree with your reality. The goal for validation is to describe your *own* reality and be understood by the third party.

If you are choosing to be validated by a third party, choose wisely. It's best not to involve someone who knows the other person. This limits damage to their relationship by not putting them in the middle.

Keep in mind that you are describing your reality and how you felt. Leave the other person's reality out of it. That way you will avoid complaining and only be seeking validation.

2. Expression

Create music, write a poem, paint an image, mold some clay, dance, write or journal, or do another form of art to express how you're feeling. Expressing emotions helps you process them. Sometimes we have really feel-good and positive emotions that we can't wait to share with the world through expression! Other times expression can be our way of giving our brains the time to process and come to terms with distressing emotions.

3. Distraction

It's okay to not want to sit with your emotions right after a conversation. If you need to, switch gears for a while, and then come back to reflect on the conversation. Garden, watch a TV comedy or a funny movie, listen to music, or read a book. Kick it up a notch by involving someone else in playing a video game, doing a puzzle, or performing other mentally engaging activities. Then, when you are ready, circle back to how you feel and use the other emotional self-care techniques listed above. When it comes to emotional self-care, a balance between expression/processing time and distraction time is the healthiest way to go!

Logistical Self-Care

Logistical self-care is about what you did and what you want to do. It is a more practical lens from which to view post-conversation self-care.

1. Reflect

Reflection is deliberate mental processing of conversations or events. Walk, run, sit quietly, or do another secondary activity while you take deliberate time to think through what you need to. Think back on the situation, ask yourself questions about it, or analyze it from other viewpoints. For example:

1. What might I do differently next time? Is troubleshooting needed?
2. I'll get a different perspective on the conversation by speaking with someone else.

Be open to different interpretations of what happened to help you understand the other person's reality. There might be more than two perspectives about what happened.

2. Give Yourself Credit

Remember the Credit Exercise from the last chapter? Here, we deliberately point out the things we did well in a conversation. Reflect, and ask things like:

1. What did *I* do well in the conversation?
2. What helped set me up for success that I can replicate next time I have a difficult or emotionally intense conversation?
3. Give yourself credit (a reward or praise) for the things you did well.

Physical Self-Care

As we learned earlier, we feel emotions physically, and that's why they're called *feel*ings! If you have had an emotionally intense conversation, it can be a great idea to bring in a physical component of self-care.

1. Safety

If needed, go somewhere you feel physically and emotionally safe. When you're feeling very unsafe or in immediate danger, do not remain isolated; call on a teacher, parent, trusted friend, or even first responders, if necessary. When you feel unsafe, your body is working hard to remain vigilant and on the lookout. Once you are somewhere safe, your body can relax.

2. Ground and Relax

Sometimes our bodies need a little extra help getting to a state where we feel calm. Use techniques from Chapter 3 ("Calm Down (Enough)") to ground and relax, such as box breathing or the Five Senses exercise, or try a guided meditation from the Internet.

3. Move and Express Yourself Physically

Cry, punch a pillow, dance, exercise, sing, or do any other safe activity that allows you to physically express emotions through movement.

Spiritual Self-Care

Depending on your beliefs, spiritual self-care may also be a category to consider. If you are a member of a religious or spiritual practice community, it's likely that there are resources available there for self-care and restoration.

"I'm Fine, I Don't Need Self-Care"

Feeling fine? I encourage you to do self-care anyway! You might mentally or physically feel fine, but subtle things happen to us when we are stressed. You literally have nothing to lose by taking care of yourself!

PRACTICE MAKES ~~PERFECT~~ EASIER

It can be hard to start a new self-care habit when our minds, our schedules, and/or our lives are already full! Therefore, I suggest creating a consistent self-care practice before you need one. Choose suggestions from the categories presented in this chapter, or make up your own self-care ideas, then add them to your weekly schedule. Write or type them into your personal or shared household calendar. (If you can't find space, this is a clue that self-care will soon be needed!) You might take walks where you can think about your day, go biking, have a hot bath, go to the gym, or do some journaling. Whatever you choose, challenge yourself to stick to a realistic, consistent schedule. That way, when life gets more intense, self-care will be built in, and you won't need to stress about adding it!

BOTTOM LINE

Taking care of yourself after an emotionally intense conversation is helpful for processing what happened; it will help you relax, move on, and learn from the experience. Prepare what you can before difficult conversations so you have a built-in cushion of support once you are finished communicating. Try out various self-care ideas and routines until you find what works for you; integrate it into your schedule for when unexpected stressors arise.

PART II

HAVING DIFFICULT CONVERSATIONS SKILLFULLY

INTRODUCTION

Welcome to Part II! In the rest of the book, I will lay out full scenarios and stories to show you how to use the ten skills you have just learned. Think of yourself like a carpenter who wants to build a beautiful rocking chair. You have just acquired ten new tools, and you know how to use each of them individually—but what do you do first, and how do you use the tools specifically for building rocking chair parts? And what do you do if something doesn't go as perfectly as planned?

In Part II, you'll see the Ten Skills of Communication applied all together in real-life stories. I'll also provide common scenarios that come up in "less than perfect" situations (i.e., real life!). Then I'll show how you can use your new tools to do something extremely important—set boundaries! You'll also learn how to use the tools to skillfully end a relationship that's no longer serving you.

After reading Part II, you will understand how the structure of the ten skills can provide a framework for difficult conversations (and, in some cases, how the skills can be used on their own) to give you confidence in handling any situation that comes up! Increased confidence will allow you to have the communication you need to build and maintain healthy relationships, creating a happier life!

Chapter 11

STORIES OF THE
TEN SKILLS IN ACTION

INTRODUCTION

In Part I, we learned and practiced the Ten Skills of Communication. Now let's apply those skills to some actual scenarios! In this chapter, I'll present five real-life stories where people used the ten skills (or, in one personal story, how I *wish* I had used them).

"HE'S NOT LISTENING!"

Max and Berner had just bought a little fishing boat together. Max was putting things away, and Berner was figuring out the navigation system. Max told him where everything was stored: life jackets under this seat, flare gun under that seat, and towels somewhere else. Then about five minutes later, Berner asked, "Where are the life jackets?"

Needless to say, Max was extremely annoyed!

In *Max's* reality, Berner obviously hadn't heard anything he had said, probably because Berner didn't look away from the navigation screen when Max was explaining where everything was. Max's Automatic Thoughts were "He doesn't listen; he doesn't respect what I say!" However, in *Berner's* reality, Max's instructions had caught him at a bad time, and Max wasn't saying anything important.

So, fighting the strong urge to say, "Why don't you ever listen!?" Max used the ten communication skills he'd learned:

1. Set Personal Goals

For Max to let Berner in on how he was feeling and describe his reality with the intention of being understood.

2. Choose a Time, Place, and Platform

On the boat, in person (but only after Max had calmed down a bit).

3. Calm Down (Enough)

Max took some deep, slow, paced breaths.

4. Remember to Listen

Max reminded himself to give Berner time to react to his statements.

5. State Common Goals

Max said, "We both want to feel heard in this relationship."

6. Validate

Max said, "I see that you're busy with the navigation system."

7. Describe

Max said, "I'm feeling really frustrated right now because I just said where the life jackets were."

8. Find Solutions

Max said, "Please let me know when you're finished with that and can give me your full attention, and I'll tell you where everything is. Does that sound okay?"

Berner and Max had already worked through the Ten Skills of Communication together, so Berner was extremely familiar with the skills, and supportive, which makes these interactions easier for them both. Berner validated Max's frustration, apologized, and then gave Max his full attention.

9. Offer Positive Reinforcement

After Max showed Berner where the life jackets were he thanked Berner for listening and for giving his full attention when Max was talking.

10. Practice Self-Care

Max gave himself credit for not losing his s%$*! And then he got to relax on the boat!

Catching yourself in the moment so you don't react in a way you'll regret is difficult. However, with practice you'll get better and better at using communication skills. And the reward of more positive interactions will act as motivation to keep you practicing these skills!

SUPPORTING RELATIONSHIPS BETWEEN TWO OTHER PEOPLE

Alex came to me with a problem: Her brother Darryl had texted her boyfriend, Ravi, saying that he didn't think Ravi had done enough for Alex's birthday. Ravi was extremely angry, and Alex needed to know how to do damage control. Her first reaction was to tell Darryl to stop texting Ravi. As we have learned, this is not a realistic goal because it's trying to *directly control* Darryl's behavior, so instead I suggested the following steps:

1. Set Personal Goals

    a. To understand Darryl's reality and why he felt the need to text Ravi. Knowing why could help Darryl feel understood and therefore less defensive. Understanding Darryl's reality could also give insight into solutions.

    b. To describe how she's feeling, with the intent to motivate Darryl to change his behavior.

2. Choose a Time, Place, and Platform

Alex thought it would be best to have the conversation with Darryl in person when she saw him in the next few days. She felt it'd be best to do this without the other family members present so they wouldn't chime in with their opinions and derail the conversation.

3. Calm Down (Enough)

I suggested Alex do some things before the conversation to help her remain calm, to clarify her personal goals, and to feel set up for success in this conversation.

4. Remember to Listen

I suggested that Alex remember to really leave space for Darryl to react, to not interrupt, and to listen to what he was saying about his reality.

5. State Common Goals

For the conversation itself, I recommended Alex start with a general goal she and Darryl share, such as, "We both love each other and always have each other's backs."

6. Validate

Having a pretty good idea of Darryl's reality, Alex could go on to validate it without needing to ask many questions. "When you texted my boyfriend, you were looking out for me and making sure I had a good birthday because you care about me and my happiness, which I really appreciate." A phrase like this would let Darryl know that she understands his reality, so he'd be less likely to be defensive later.

7. Describe

Next, Alex could go on to describe her reality to Darryl, avoiding the use of the word "you." For example, "I felt put in the middle and awkward about the situation, and that was really hard for me."

8. Find Solutions

Alex could propose a solution: "I was wondering if you could help by running by me the stuff you want to text to Ravi in advance. What do you think about trying that and seeing how it goes?" This solution is framed as a way that Darryl can help Alex, and Alex asks Darryl his opinion in the form of an open-ended question. She wasn't *telling* him to do anything; she was *asking* for his help. And, since he cares about her, and they both want each other to be happy, chances are he'd be willing to help!

9. Offer Positive Reinforcement

Darryl ended up agreeing to Alex's solution, and she gave him positive reinforcement by thanking him for being open to her ideas.

10. Practice Self-Care

As part of her post-conversation self-care, Alex also created some boundaries with herself about what she would tell Darryl about her relationship with Ravi. She also had a conversation with Ravi in which she validated his anger and concern about Darryl's message. I encouraged her to also give herself credit for handling this situation so well!

WHEN I DIDN'T SET GOALS WELL

This next story happened to me and is an example of a time where I *didn't* use the skills (because I didn't know them yet), and, as a result, things did not go well. I'll tell you the story first and then do a postmortem on the situation, in which I'll show you how the skills would have made a huge difference to my communication.

When I was in college, it was standard practice for teachers and professors to hand out a feedback form on the last day of class. The professors passed out the forms and then left the room so the students could fill them out honestly, without the teacher being present. Then a student volunteer would collect all the forms, place them in a folder, and bring it to an administrator at the school's front desk. Later, the professor and program director would review the anonymous forms.

However, in one of my classes, the professor handed out the forms and then stayed in the room. She said she wanted to collect the forms to read immediately because she was going on leave the next term and so wouldn't be able to read them unless she did it right after class.

I felt *very* uncomfortable about this. I asked the professor if she would like me to bring the forms to the front desk, since that was the process other professors followed. She declined my offer and stayed in the room. I knew many of my classmates had mixed feelings about our professor, and I wondered how many students were censoring their reviews, knowing that she was present and collecting the forms herself.

After a couple days, this situation still didn't feel right to me, so I decided to reach out to Dr. Roberts, the program director. But at this point in my life, I hadn't studied communication yet, so I didn't know anything about setting goals or any of the other ten skills. So, not surprisingly, the meeting didn't go well. I started by explaining the situation (describe), and Dr. Roberts got very defensive on the professor's behalf. I began stating some values of the school (an attempt at common goals, even though I wouldn't have called it that at the time), but that only confused him. At one point Dr. Roberts even asked me, "Are you trying to get [professor's name] in trouble?" To which I wanted to reply, "What kind of person do you think I am?!" But instead I started crying, and it felt *awful.* This question was a clear sign Dr. Roberts was (very validly) confused!

I eventually realized that I just wanted the school to know what happened (describe with intent to be understood) and perhaps see if they were going to do anything to remind teachers of this important process (find solutions) to uphold the integrity of the system. By the end of the meeting, we'd gotten to these options, but it took a lot of confusion on both our parts and a lot of tears on my end to get there. I went home thinking, "What the f@#$ just happened?"

With many more years of experience (and counselor training) under my belt, I can now see why things went so poorly. I wasn't clear on my personal goals, and so Dr. Roberts was (understandably) very confused about what those goals were! If I had instead used the Ten Skills of Communication, the meeting might have looked something like this:

1. Set Personal Goals

  a. To describe the situation, and the discomfort it caused me, with intent to be understood.

    b. To find solutions by asking what could be done in future similar situations so that a teacher could get the forms quickly while still respecting student confidentiality

2. Choose a Time, Place, and Platform

This communication could have been done over email, which would probably have been better for me, as I tend to get emotionally overwhelmed when speaking with authority figures.

3. Calm Down (Enough)

I would take some time for grounding beforehand.

4. Remember to Listen

This would have been a great reminder that would have possibly helped me understand Dr. Roberts's confusion a lot sooner!

5. State Common Goals

I might have said, "We're both invested in the values and integrity of the school," rather than randomly stating school values.

6. Validate

I could validate Dr. Roberts and the professor by saying, "I understand she is going on leave and didn't think it would be a big deal to be in the room and collect the forms. I also believe that this situation might put you in a difficult position because the forms are already handed in." This statement validates both the professor and Dr. Roberts, and could potentially defuse Dr. Roberts's defensiveness.

7. Describe

"I felt awkward and uncomfortable when the professor collected the forms."

8. Find Solutions

"I'm wondering if there's anything that might be done in the future so this doesn't happen again." In this example, Dr. Roberts would need to identify solutions, as he is the one with the knowledge of the current system and the power to implement changes.

9. Offer Positive Reinforcement

After we'd discussed a solution, I would thank Dr. Roberts for listening and taking the time to speak with me.

10. Practice Self-Care

As I mentioned before, I have a tough time speaking with authority figures, and this was no exception. Ideally, I would have set up a phone call with a friend during my walk home, so that I could get my reality validated in case Dr. Roberts wasn't able to do that. I would also give myself credit for the things I felt I did well in the conversation.

Of course, the hypothetical seems great on paper, but I can't say for sure how it would have gone in real life. All I know is that I feel it would have been *a lot* smoother had I known to identify personal goals to clarify why I was going in to talk with Dr. Roberts and what I was hoping to get out of the conversation!

ANNOYING WORK EMAILS

One Sunday evening, Tim got an email from his boss, Adelina. She wanted all staff to change their work hours (9 a.m. to 5 p.m.) to a new schedule of 10 a.m. to 6 p.m. Tim's initial reaction was anger; he didn't want to work the newly proposed hours because it would cut into his fishing time and other after-work plans (but mostly the fishing!). He wanted to write back to Adelina and say "Weekend ruiner!" Instead, I suggested the following plan to him.

1. Set Personal Goals

a. Understand the purpose of the change. This can be helpful in coming up with solutions.

b. Describe his frustration and inability to make the new hours work, with the intent to motivate the boss to find another solution that works within the 9-to-5 workday.

2. Choose a Time, Place, and Platform

Tim could reply by email later in the evening or have a conversation in person the next day.

3. Calm Down (Enough)

For Tim, this meant taking time to cool down and do some other activities before sending a reply.

4. Remember to Listen

During email (or text) conversations, this is a lot easier to achieve and might not need such a direct reminder.

5. State Common Goals

"We both want the company to succeed, and we both want a positive work relationship and environment."

6. Validate

Tim could validate that Adelina wants to change the hours. He could also get curious as to why the hours are getting changed and perhaps validate that reason. (As it turned out, Adelina wanted all employees to be present at a new 5 p.m. daily meeting.)

7. Describe

Tim could then explain his reality: he feels stressed and burdened by a schedule change and its impact on other commitments.

8. Find Solutions

Propose the meetings be held at 4 p.m. instead or be held virtually at 5 p.m. Tim could ask Adelina for feedback and if those options are viable.

9. Offer Positive Reinforcement

Tim would thank Adelina for listening to him and his suggestions, and for coming up with a solution to try.

10. Practice Self-Care

Tim would go fishing while waiting for a reply.

Tim took some of my suggestions but not all of them. He used the Ten Skills of Communication and came up with language that felt comfortable to him and that fit his personality and what he knew about Adelina's personality. I'm happy to say that Tim and Adelina were able to come up with the solution that Tim could attend the meetings virtually!

MANAGING HOUSEHOLD CHORES

Who does the household chores (and how and when) is a hot topic in any home. Aaliyah came to me with this issue. Her roommates, Van and Jamal, never tidied up their common living/eating space, and she felt like she was always picking up after them and like she was the only one doing chores like cleaning the bathroom. We talked through the situation and together came up with a plan for her to apply the Ten Skills of Communication to a conversation with Van and Jamal.

1. Set Personal Goals

   a. To describe her emotions around Van and Jamal not helping to keep the house clean.
   b. To come up with solutions to help with household chores.

2. Choose a Time, Place, and Platform

Aaliyah and I decided the best time to bring up a conversation was when the three roommates were all in decent moods and had the time to give the conversation their full attention. Aaliyah would *not* bring it up if she was currently frustrated about a mess or an untidy space.

3. Calm Down (Enough)

Running was a tool Aaliyah used to calm down and reduce stress, so she decided she'd go for a run before the conversation.

4. Remember to Listen

I reminded Aaliyah to listen to Van's and Jamal's reactions, giving them her full attention, and not to be distracted by her phone or other devices.

5. State Common Goals

Aaliyah came up with some options: "We all want to live in a place where we respect each other," or "We all want as positive an environment as possible."

6. Validate

"You're both really busy, and so sometimes you don't have time to clean up our space, or you say you will do it later but then forget. You don't seem to mean any harm or stress to me by leaving dishes in the sink or the bathroom dirty."

7. Describe

"For me, it's really frustrating to not be able to come home to a clean house. It doesn't seem like your intention, but it leaves me feeling really disrespected."

This describing example includes a validation, to help fend off any defensiveness from Jamal or Van. This example also keeps attention on the feelings, rather than bringing up specific "evidence" of the dishes not being done.

8. Find Solutions

"What do you think are some ways we can help change this situation so we can all feel better about living together? Could we each have our own set of dishes and only use and clean our own? Or maybe one of us does the dishes, but the other one cleans the floors and bathroom and other common spaces?" Aaliyah would stay open to other ideas her roommates had, so together they could come up with a temporary solution to see how it went.

9. Offer Positive Reinforcement

"Thank you so much for listening to me. I really appreciate it!"

10. Practice Self-Care

Aaliyah made plans to go out with a good friend after the conversation in case she needed help reflecting on the situation or getting some validation her roommates might not have been able to give her.

PRACTICE MAKES ~~PERFECT~~ EASIER

Start to practice the ten skills by playing a situation out in your head while going through the skills. It can be a situation you are going to be in soon or have already experienced. Look at each skill individually, in order, and think about how each could be applied to your situation.

Worried you'll forget a skill in the moment? There are Communication Skills Checklists (pages 264 and 266) in Appendices III and IV; take a photo so you have the skills handy even if you don't have this book with you. For more about using the skills on their own, check out Chapter 12.

It may sound funny, but I often suggest that clients watch reality television to practice the skills of communication. Reality TV often features a lot of conflict (otherwise it'd be super boring!), and you can use the skills you've learned to pinpoint what went wrong and why! Typically, in reality TV, there is a lot of describing and imposing of realities, and not a lot of listening and validating. Have fun with this—invite your partner or family or friends to join you, order takeout, and turn on your favorite reality show. See who can compile the greatest number of obstacles and solutions. Consider:

- What could the people in the show have done or said to communicate more effectively?
- What common goals do they share?
- What might be their personal goals?
- What might be their Automatic Thoughts in a certain situation?
- Are their personal goals fair, realistic, and achievable?
- Are they validating each other or only describing their reality?
- Are they willing to compromise to find solutions? What are some compromises you can think of?
- How might you validate each of their realities?
- At the end of the conversation, have they reached their goals?
- How do things end?
- Do they end up having a similar argument later because the issue was not resolved?

CONCLUSION

With practice, the Ten Skills of Communication will become easier to remember and a natural part of how you communicate. As seen in the previous examples, the skills can be used as a structure to outline conversations so they go smoothly and you can achieve your goals. Chapter 13 will also help in highlighting the skills of communication in common difficult scenarios.

Chapter 12

USING SKILLS ON THEIR OWN

INTRODUCTION

Not ready to have a direct conversation about something? No problem! There might be a circumstance where you feel either you aren't prepared to have a direct conversation—or the other person might not be in the right state of mind to be receptive, and that's okay! In this chapter, we'll review the skills of communication that are great stand-alone tools for indirectly addressing personal goals without having a formal, direct conversation.

USING SKILLS ON THEIR OWN: WHY IT'S IMPORTANT

Indirectly addressing personal goals can be important to gaining confidence in your communication skills. Practicing some of the skills on their own, rather than in a structured conversation, can help you feel a lot more comfortable with them. Addressing goals indirectly can also be very useful if the other person is being defensive or if you are too anxious or nervous to jump right into a direct conversation. Though I don't want to promote avoidance, indirect addressing of goals can be a great middle step on the way to directly addressing issues.

USING SKILLS ON THEIR OWN: HOW TO DO IT

You can indirectly "test the waters" using some of the stand-alone skills described below.

Positive Reinforcement

As we know, positive reinforcement is a very useful stand-alone tool. I often assign this as homework in my first couples therapy sessions. As discussed, it gives a clear sense of what behaviors you want, which is especially important because we can't always assume people know what they're doing that's working well.

- "I'm really happy that you were able to share that with me; thank you."
- "I really appreciate the acknowledgment of my work and what you appreciate about the effort I put in, and that you gave me constructive feedback in a respectful way."

Positive reinforcement can create shifts toward your goals without having to directly discuss them.

Stating Common Goals

This tool introduces the long-term goals you are both working toward. Simply communicating these positive ideas can plant seeds in the other person's mind of where you'd like changes to be made or where you want the relationship to go.

- "I'd love to have more talks about the future, since we both seem to want this relationship to move forward."
- "It seems like we're both into getting this project done on time and in the best way possible. That's great—we're on the same team!"

Combining common goals and positive reinforcement can be especially effective!

- "I appreciate you opening up to me, and I'd love to have more conversations like this about managing our child's behavior."

Stating common goals on their own can also help ensure you are on the same page. Putting them out into conversation and then noticing the reaction of the other person can tell you a lot about whether your values and goals align. And if you can reach goals together with little effort, all the better!

Finally, stating common goals is a great stand-alone tool because it doesn't always require a larger conversation to follow. For example, imagine if every time your partner said, "We both love each other and want each other to be happy," to you, it was followed by an intense conversation. You would want there to be times it was "We both love each other and want each other to be happy" and nothing more—otherwise, every time you hear "We both love each other and want each other to be happy," you're waiting for the other shoe to drop, and you don't really take in the positive sentiment. So, state common goals often! Think of them as little positive reminders that you're on the same team.

Validation (of Others and Self)

Validating someone else can be a very powerful way to model the behavior you'd like to see from them. Over time, consistent, sincere validation can help someone soften and become less defensive because they are feeling very understood, which will lessen their urge to jump in and defend their reality. Remember that, even if the other person is not able or ready to reciprocate, your reality is still valid; try using the tools discussed previously to get that validation elsewhere (talking to a friend, family member, or counselor, or journaling, for instance).

Working Independently on Personal Goals

Consider what your personal goals are in a relationship, and start working toward them on your own. For example, if someone is pulling away but you are wanting to communicate more, your first reaction may be to also pull away. Instead, lean into communicating: listen first, be curious, and validate their experience. You can even ask for help if the situation warrants it.

- "I'm really working to emotionally regulate during our family get-togethers."
- "It sounds like you've got a lot going on. I'd like to understand more about your work stress. What's been happening?"
- "I'm working on staying calm and not getting defensive during conversations about my illness. Are you willing to gently point that out to me next time you notice it?" (This will only work if you're ready to receive those corrections in the moment.)

Becoming more aware of goals in any type of interaction can be great practice for higher-intensity conversations.

Staying Calm

The importance of this skill is obvious, yet it can be a difficult one to master. When we are feeling invalidated or personally attacked, our instinct is often to act out or react in ways we'll regret later. Practice the calming techniques described in this book until they become a habit. You'll find that grounding and calming will not only help you with difficult conversations but in many other scenarios as well.

CONCLUSION

The Ten Skills of Communication are a recipe; you can use them as directed in Part I, or you can change, subtract, or add what suits your taste. Think of the skills listed above as stand-alone "appetizers" or "snacks." Practicing any of the skills of communication can help you feel more confident in your abilities foster positivity, and move you toward your relationship goals, even if you're not directly having a full conversation!

Chapter 13

HANDLING DIFFICULT
EVERYDAY SCENARIOS
SKILLFULLY

INTRODUCTION

Let's be real: sometimes things don't go as planned! So now that you've seen the Ten Skills of Communication in action, I'll outline some common derailing scenarios I get asked about by client and make recommendations for how they (and you) can use a combination of skills to manage them. You'll learn how to skillfully handle difficult communication scenarios such as victim mentality, bullying, jokes gone wrong, and more!

SWITCHING TOPICS, OR VICTIM MENTALITY

Clients ask me this a lot: "What can I do when the other person starts making it all about them?" It can be extremely difficult to stick to your conversation goal if the other person has their own agenda. They might bring up something unrelated or try to make it about how they're now feeling bad. Either way, they're derailing the conversation, leading it away from your personal goals and toward themself. To manage this, it's first important to understand why this happens. People often derail conversations for the following reasons:

1. *They've had something to say but didn't bring it up, so they are using this as an opportunity to air their own thoughts and feelings.* This often comes up when people have "stuffed things down" or "bottled things up" (which is

why it's best not to do those things, despite confrontation being difficult for some!).

2. *It is too uncomfortable for them to admit they've caused any discomfort*, as it does not align with the intentions in their own reality. They are hurt by seeing you hurt and so need to distract from that to validate their own reality and intentions.

3. *They feel that even admitting to unintentionally causing distress in someone else makes them a "bad person."* Becoming the victim makes you the "bad person" instead, or at the very least redirects the attention away from them. Now they are the one being taken care of or attended to, which can be much more comfortable.

If someone is bringing up topics unrelated to your goals or turns themself into a victim, you have three options:

1. Validate and resolve their issue first.

Reflect their emotions, and use your describing, validating, and solution-finding skills as needed. Once the issue is resolved, circle back to your original goal.

- "You seem really hurt by me bringing up this topic. Can you explain a bit more about why it's hurting you? I'd love to know more about your perspective."

2. Validate, then gently redirect.

Reflect their emotions, and state that they seem important for them to bring up, but that you want to discuss your topic and resolve it first—and then you'll be happy to circle back around. You can even offer to write down their topic, especially if multiple other topics are coming up.

- "It seems as though you're feeling really hurt about the topic I brought up. How about we first talk about the topic, because it's important to me that we find solutions to try, and then we can work at helping you feel better?"

3. Close the conversation, or move straight to solution-finding.

If that's needed and part of the goals. (There is more about shutting things down at the end of this chapter.)

"It seems like we're getting a bit derailed here and we're both feeling hurt. Let's take a break and come back to this later this evening after dinner."

"It seems like we're getting a bit derailed here and we're both feeling hurt. Let's think of some solutions so we can wrap this topic up as efficiently as possible."

WHEN THEIR REACTION IS NOT WHAT YOU EXPECTED OR INTENDED

Since we all operate in different realities, sometimes people will interpret what you do and say to mean something different from what you intended or expected. Think about The Dress. It's actually a wonder we can get anything done! If you find yourself in a situation where you have been misinterpreted, you may have the urge to defend your reality. But first, you must validate! Follow the steps below to help ease into describing your reality and intentions when the reaction was not what you expected. In the next sections, I'll touch on specific kinds of reactions (like anger and crying).

1. First, validate how they feel.

If you don't know, ask! Get curious as to why they were offended or hurt; was it your tone? Or maybe something about the situation reminded them of a similar situation from the past? Finding out *why* can help you avoid being in the same position in the future.

- "You seem shocked about what I just said; I'm curious what's going on for you right now. How are you feeling about this news?"
- "The comment I just made seems to have offended you. Am I getting that right?"
- "How did you interpret what I just said?"

Asking open-ended questions can give them the space to explain their reality.

2. Next, describe your reality.

Once they feel understood, describe your reality. State your actual intentions, and apologize for the confusion.

- "I'm sorry that news shocked you. There seems to have been some miscommunication, and I'm feeling confused as to what's going on for you right now because I thought you'd be happy about this."
- "I'm sorry you felt offended; my intention was for that comment to be funny. I feel awful that you were hurt by that."

Notice how these examples aren't explaining how they "should not" have felt but rather how you intended they would feel. Telling them that their reaction was "incorrect" can potentially lead to more defensiveness. Look at the table below for some examples of how you can clarify your intention in a non-imposing way. Notice the trend of "you" statements in the imposing language and "I" statements in the non-imposing language:

Imposing Description of Intent	Non-Imposing Description of Intent
"You weren't meant to be hurt."	"I meant that as a compliment."
"You weren't supposed to get confused by that."	"My intention was to be clear, so I'm sorry if that wasn't the case."
"You were supposed to know I was joking."	"I thought you'd think that was funny."

3. Last, find solutions.

What can you do differently in the future? Perhaps change your tone, avoid joking about certain subjects, or be gentler when it comes to certain topics?

- "In the future, can we think of a better way for me to bring things up so they won't alarm you as much?"
- "I'm thinking in the future I will be gentler when talking about this because I don't want to offend you. Any ideas that can help me do that?"

INTENSE EMOTIONAL REACTIONS AND ESCALATION—YELLING, ANGER, AND MORE!

When things heat up and emotions become dysregulated, the conversation can get out of hand and goals thrown out the window. This can look like yelling or even physical or emotional abuse. First, be safe. Remove yourself from any situation where you are being abused an any way. If someone is having a very intense reaction, but you are still safe, it is time to (you guessed it) validate!

Switching between describing and validating is expected because managing the *reaction* to your reality will often require validation.

You can also try to co-regulate. As presented earlier, in Chapter 3 ("Calm Down (Enough)"), co-regulating means working to stay calm yourself. This is challenging, but if you've been practicing your techniques of breathing and grounding during most of your conversations, it will be "front of brain" and come to you quickly.

Yelling is something I hear about often from clients. If we think about why yelling is happening, we can help make it stop. Why do people yell? In most cases, it is a very literal reaction to feeling unheard. If you don't feel like someone is listening to you or understanding you, or hearing you you increase the volume! Keep this in mind when you're having conversations. If you notice that the other person is beginning to raise their voice (or you catch yourself doing it), that is your alarm system to switch to validating or to use the describing tips from this book to be clear and concise so you are easy to understand.

Anger is another common extreme emotion my clients talk about. Though it's in the same arena as yelling, it can have a different cause. If we know more about the cause of anger, we can cut it off at the source.

How do children or pets react when someone gets angry with them? They usually get scared. We become angry in order to scare others because, on some level (whether conscious or subconscious), we are trying to protect ourselves. Dialectical Behavior Therapy (DBT)[7] holds that there are three reasons why we have emotions: to communicate to ourselves, to communicate to others, and to create action. Anger is an emotion that comes out when our resources are being threatened. It's communicating to others that we feel threatened in some way. Resources can be anything—they are often physical things such as items or people—but resources can also be our emotions. Often angry people are trying to protect themselves from being hurt. If someone is deeply hurting you, you want them to back off, so you become angry to "scare" them away. The thing about this is, as adults, most of us aren't so afraid of anger that we back away and cower like a pet dog might. The next time you or someone else gets angry, it can be another alarm bell that prompts you to consider: What resource is being threatened here? Why am I/the other person trying to protect or defend myself/themself? Use the cognitive model. What Automatic Thoughts are coming up that are causing an emotional reaction of anger? Reminding yourself that you are safe and you are able to protect whatever resource feels threatened might allow you to have a different reaction than anger.

If you or the other person is not able to stay calm (enough) to have a conversation, then it might be time to pause the conversation and come back to it at a different time. There is more on how to do that later in this chapter.

IF SOMEONE STARTS CRYING

Crying often seems to be wrapped in shame. We try not to cry, or we don't want to be around other people crying, and we generally think it's not a great thing. If I were in charge, I would change this! Crying is normal, and it can even allow us to reach a different place emotionally. Think about what we just learned about emotions as a means of communication. *Crying helps us communicate to ourselves and others how we're feeling*, which can be really helpful!

If you are a frequent crier, I'm right there with you. Rarely a week goes by where I haven't cried at least once from being frustrated, angry, or even overwhelmed with joy; it really doesn't take much. Sometimes it even happens when I'm speaking to an authority figure, and, boy, do I wish I could control it!

If you notice you cry in certain situations, it might be worth having conversations beforehand, or you can communicate during the talk about what is going on when you are crying. Crying might cause the other person to feel at a loss as to what to do, so being direct can be very helpful. Or discuss how you'd like to handle it when it does come up. For example:

- "When I cry, it seems like you feel really helpless as to what to do. Usually, I just want to finish the conversation. So if it's okay with you, what do you think about trying that next time?"
- "I get upset and start crying, and then my thoughts get jumbled, which seems like it's really confusing for you. Next time that happens, how would you feel about taking five minutes to regroup and then keep the conversation going?"

In these examples, you'll notice that the discomfort of the person who is *not* crying is being validated. If the plan is to take some time, there are also specific plans suggested to come back to reach the goals of the conversation. If you are in a situation where you are crying and haven't talked about what to do, try one of the following phrases:

- "I am upset about what happened and how hurt I am, but I'd like to keep talking about things. How do you feel about continuing?"

- "I'm crying because I'm feeling overwhelmed. How would you feel if I took a few minutes to breathe, and then we came back to this topic?"

Notice there are no apologies in these examples. If you want to, you can of course add an apology, but I personally don't agree with apologizing for expressing emotion in a healthy way. Apologizing for crying further perpetuates the stigma around crying or expressing emotion. I have people try to "hold it in" or apologize to me for it in a counseling session, but I see people cry all day! It breaks my heart that even in *an environment literally meant to express emotions,* clients still feel the need to apologize for crying. I say, let it flow!

What should you do if it's the other person who is crying and you are on the receiving end? Seeing someone else cry can leave us feeling helpless, out of control, uncomfortable, guilty, and "bad" ourselves.

The first urge can be to get them to stop crying because managing your own discomfort takes over, and that's a very valid reaction! However, getting them to stop by shutting the conversation down or by taking care of them would be veering away from the conversation goals. So, when someone starts crying, give them time and go slow; we all know it's hard to talk while crying! Slow things down and speak gently. You can ask them how they're feeling, or if there's anything they want to do. They might just want to finish the conversation; they might want to take some time on their own to regroup. If your own discomfort level is too high, then you can be the one who asks to take some time, and plan to come back to the conversation later. Work as a team to come up with solutions and compromises you are both comfortable with.

MANAGING EXTREME DEFENSIVENESS

Despite your best efforts, some people will still take your description of your reality as an attack. For whatever reason, they will have their walls and their guard up, and it can seem impossible to have a productive conversation. People can be defensive for many reasons. Sometimes you've got their reality wrong, which creates in them a sense of being falsely accused, and sometimes they're just used to being misunderstood all the time. Sometimes they aren't ready to admit they're feeling a certain way because of what they think that says about them as a person. Whatever the reason, to manage extreme defensiveness, you can *try to validate.* How are they feeling? Ask for clarification if necessary, then validate by using the same language they've used. This often works, but sometimes, no matter what you do, people are not able to accept their own feelings about a topic or are out to disagree with anything that is said, even if it's accurate.

Speaker A: "Sounds like you had a bad day."

Speaker B: "No, it was just normal. Weren't you listening? That's so annoying!"

Speaker A: "Sorry you feel like I wasn't listening; it's annoying to feel like someone isn't listening."

Speaker B: "Yeah, that is really annoying." (validation acceptance)

or

Speaker B: "I'm not annoyed!" (validation defense)

You can see here that Speaker B is probably going to disagree with any validation Speaker A offers. If the other person is not accepting validation, you can keep trying, move to solution-finding if that's needed for your goals, or choose to shut the conversation down.

- *Keep trying:* "Seems like I'm not understanding you well. Can you please try to explain to me what's going on for you?"
- *Move to finding solutions:* "Sounds like you had a bad day; that really sucks. Would you be okay with changing the subject and talking about

what we're going to do this evening? Maybe that will help take your mind off your day."

- *Shut down the conversation:* "Sounds like you had a bad day. Do you want some time to decompress, and we can talk in a bit?"

CONVERSATIONS WITH BULLIES

Bullies are not only found on the playground. They're also grown-ups, alive and doing their thing in adult life! I know because I used to work very closely with one, which was a difficult and confusing experience. In adult life, bullying might be more subtle but can still involve name-calling, putting other people down, and unproductive negativity with the intent to hurt someone. Bullies intentionally try to hurt, harm, and invalidate others. It can help to know that underneath a bully's cruel behavior is often someone who is hurting and confused or who has been bullied themselves. However, just because a bully is reacting to their own pain does not mean their behavior is excusable or okay.

As we know, you cannot make anyone behave the way you want them to, and that is not the purpose of this book. You can take care of yourself, though, regardless of someone else's actions. When you are dealing with a bully, try the following:

1. Stay calm

This can be hard. Use the skills you learned in Chapter 3 ("Calm Down (Enough)") to help.

2. Validate

Get curious about what they might have been trying to achieve with their behavior.

- "Can you help me understand a bit more about how you're feeling?"

- "I'm feeling a bit confused. Could you please explain more about what happened, from your perspective?"

3. Describe

Then (potentially) describe how their behavior makes you feel, although this might be a time when it will not be understood or validated. If so, you might need to get your reality validated elsewhere—or move straight to solution-finding if that's the goal of the conversation.

> Speaker A (the bully): "That person is so lazy and terrible at their job."
>
> Speaker B: "You seem frustrated by their performance. Why is that frustrating for you?"
>
> Speaker A: "I'm not frustrated."
>
> Speaker B: "How are you feeling?"
>
> Speaker A: "Angry; they just don't work hard."
>
> Speaker B: "Oh, so you're feeling angry that to you it seems they don't work hard."
>
> Speaker A: (doesn't respond)
>
> Speaker B: "That sucks that you're feeling so angry. I want to let you know, though, that I feel uncomfortable when comments are made about how other people work when they're not around to speak for themselves."

4. Set a boundary

To indicate that you will not make mean remarks or respond to what you perceive as bullying, use the boundary-setting steps in Chapter 14.

- "It'd really help me out if we could talk about work stuff instead of other people. How do you feel about that?"

5. Rethink the goals or even the relationship

If the bully is still being mean in your presence (or mean to you personally), then it might be time to end the relationship (see Chapter 15). If you will still need to have a relationship with them (for example, they're a work colleague or family member), then you can do two things. First, model the behavior you want to see. Don't be a bully yourself! Second, avoid reinforcing their bullying behaviors. If they make a comment, say nothing. Pretend they didn't say it. In other words, ignore it. Switch the topic entirely. Doing this doesn't give them attention by agreeing, disagreeing, or punishing. Whatever their motive for bullying, having a completely neutral reaction will hopefully help extinguish the behavior by not feeding it.

CONVERSATION AVOIDANCE

You might have been able to get to the validate or describe steps with someone, only to find that they are avoiding continuing the conversation.

- "I don't want to talk about this."
- "Do we need to go there?"
- "This isn't important."
- Or giving short, one-word answers and not engaging in the conversation: "Yeah," "Fine," "Whatever."

If someone is avoiding a conversation, you can have a new conversation using the applicable communication skills with the personal goal of understanding why they are avoiding the topic. Then you can find solutions so you both feel more comfortable having the conversation. For example, does someone else need to be present, do they need to take breaks if they get overwhelmed, or do they need the conversation to happen at a different, specific time/place? You can also use the skills with the personal goal of describing with the intent to be understood (about how important it is to you to have the conversation).

- "It seems like you don't want to talk, but I am feeling really confused about this. Would it be okay if we talk about this later this evening, once we've had some time to think about it?"
- "This topic can be really uncomfortable, but it's important to me as I am feeling hurt by the situation. What would help you feel more comfortable talking about this?"
- "You sound really busy and stressed, like this conversation may not be a priority. For me, I'm having a tough time and feeling saddened by the situation. What do you think about finding a time next week that would work for you to talk about this?"

Notice how these examples validate the other person's discomfort and offer help in the form of questions about solutions. The actual conversation topic has been set aside for now, and the current topic is their discomfort with the situation. Hopefully, once this is addressed, you can circle back to your original goals.

JOKES GONE WRONG

Reactions aren't always as we intended, especially when it comes to jokes. We can feel really bad when a joke not only doesn't land but also has offended someone. When a joke goes wrong, the joke-teller might react this way:

- "Oh my gosh, I'm so sorry—I was just joking."
- "That was just a joke."

This language will probably work much of the time, but if you want to step it up a bit more, you can try:

- "You were hurt by what I just said. I'm so sorry. I meant it as a joke, and I won't joke about that anymore."

In this example, there is validation before the apology. This can be helpful in opening the other person up to accept the apology because they'll know you understand how they feel through the validation you gave them.

Another urge people might have in this situation is to say something like:

- "Oh, come on, I was just joking; don't be upset."

As we know by this point, here the joke-teller is imposing their reality on the receiver. In the teller's reality, the joke was appropriate and not intended to hurt anyone. But in the receiver's reality, the joke was inappropriate and hurtful. The teller is defending their reality, probably because they feel bad. Hopefully the teller in this situation can recognize that they (accidentally!) hurt someone and accept that other realities exist, including reactions different from the ones intended.

If you are the receiver, you can use the same strategies as when you deal with someone who makes "you shouldn't feel that way" comments (see page 105)—that is, validate their intention in *their* reality, then concisely describe how you feel. As stated before, it's not the end of the world if someone is hurt or uncomfortable, so telling them how you feel is valid and fair (if done respectfully). Doing this will help you both build confidence in the skills to understand each other, find solutions, and move on!

WHEN THEY KEEP "ONE-UPPING"

This is similar to the situation in which the person turns the conversation back to themself, either making themselves "more of a victim" or "better than you," depending on what you're talking about. Here are some examples where Speaker B "one-ups" Speaker A:

Speaker A: "I didn't get home until 5:00 today!"

Speaker B: "I never get home by 5:00; I always work late."

Speaker A: "I had a really great pizza the other day."

Speaker B: "I once had the best pizza in Italy."

This can be extremely frustrating. You are trying to describe your reality with the intent to be understood, yet the other person is invalidating you, perhaps without even realizing it. There are a few things you can do here.

1. As always, validate the other person's experience.

This can be very difficult when you yourself were just invalidated, but it can open them up to your experience, which will come again later.

- "You work really long hours and don't get home until late."
- "That's really cool that you went to Italy and had really good pizza."

(Tone here is very important; you don't want to come across as sarcastic or patronizing.)

2. Next, try describing again, more clearly.

- "You work really long hours and don't get home until really late in the day; for me, 5:00 is a lot later than usual, and so I feel like I had a really long day."
- "That's really cool you went to Italy and had really good pizza! I also had really good pizza. It was the highlight of my day and made me feel really happy!"

3. Last, if you really want to curb this pattern, employ immediacy, explaining what you want from them.

- "You work really long hours and don't get home until late; for me, 5:00 is a lot later than usual. I am trying to let you know that I also had a really long day."
- "That's really cool that you went to Italy and had really good pizza. And I was also wanting to share with you that I had really good pizza, because it was the highlight of my day, and so I would really appreciate you acknowledging that."

If you notice one-upping is an ongoing issue, you may want to do some boundary-setting around this. Work with your personal goals for the conversation. You most likely are in a position where you want to describe with the intent to be understood. Ask yourself: can you work together with the other person to help extinguish their invalidating behavior and replace it with some validation *before* their own storytelling?

THEY KEEP ASKING THE SAME QUESTION

Sometimes we feel as though we can't move on in the conversation because the same question keeps being brought up. There are a few reasons why this usually happens.

The first is that the person did not get the answer they wanted, so they are (consciously or even unconsciously) asking it again and again in hopes of getting their desired response. Another reason asking the same question happens is that the person did not understand the answer, so they are looking for clarity.

Being asked multiple times to do a favor you said no to already can look like this:

- "Are you sure you can't just do me this favor though? It's not a big ask!"
- "But the favor won't take too long, so you should be able to do it, right?"
- "Okay, but you did it last time, so you should be able to do it this time."

And on and on and on. . . .

To manage this situation, the first step is to be aware that it is happening. A good signal is that you will feel frustrated and/or stalled in the conversation. The next step is to validate and try to understand the other person's reality.

- "Are you feeling at all confused about my answer to your question?"
- "Is there anything I can explain better to help you understand?"

(Tone here is very important; you need to sound genuine and not condescending.)

Validate their confusion or disappointment in your answer.

- "I mentioned that I was not able to do that favor for you, and that seems like it was a big disappointment for you."
- "I mentioned that I was not able to do that favor for you, and you seem confused about why I can't do it."

Their reactions to these statements will let you know if you're on the right track. Then follow the thread that fits.

- "My intention was not to disappoint you, and it sucks to feel disappointed. How about I do [compromise], though? How would that feel?"
- "I feel overwhelmed by my schedule right now and so am not able to get that done for you. I can see how that might be confusing since I was able to do it last time."

These reflections should help with feeling understood so you can move past the question being asked repeatedly and on to solution-finding and a peaceful end to the conversation.

If the person is relentless with their repeated questioning, it might be time to set up a healthy boundary around being asked this question again.

See Chapter 14 for more information on communicating boundaries and setting up repercussions if boundaries are crossed.

MANAGING CONSISTENT INTERRUPTING

Being interrupted can be really annoying! If you notice this pattern in your conversations, there are a few things you can do.

1. Put a pin in the interrupting.

Consider bringing up the interrupting as a separate conversation topic at another time and place, when you're calm and able to achieve some boundary-setting goals around it (see Chapter 14). Using some previously agreed-upon techniques around interrupting can be helpful as an "in the moment" plan.

2. Use immediacy and mini-goals.

If you don't have the luxury of leaving the interrupting until it can be addressed separately, the goal would be to describe with the intent to be understood and to motivate toward small goals.

- "When I'm not able to finish my sentence, I feel really frustrated because I feel like I can't fully explain what I'm trying to get across."

Notice how the word "you" is not used here. Saying to someone, "You keep interrupting me!" is accusatory and will most likely lead to the defense that they don't agree with you (they're not interrupting) or a justification (as in, "I knew what you were going to say").

3. Find solutions

Bringing the other person's awareness to their interrupting can be helpful on its own because maybe they're not even realizing they're doing it! Then, if they are willing, you can also find solutions, such as:

* "It would really help me feel better to finish a thought fully before it gets responded to."

If you are having issues with interruptions, here is a simple exercise that can help. Choose a small object, like a stone or ball, and set a conversation rule that only the person with that object can speak. Take turns passing it back and forth; this can really help to define who is the speaker and who is the listener, and when those roles shift. (You can also use it while practicing when to listen, validate, and describe. If you don't have the object, you are listening. If you have just been passed the object, you are validating or reflecting, then moving on to describing.)

WHAT IF THEY'RE JUST PLAIN WRONG?

Over the year that I was writing this book, I discussed it often with my partner. He was very helpful at testing my theories "in the field" and made it his mission to find a situation where validation was not useful and perhaps "invalidation" was needed. Remember the 2 + 2 = 5 example? That came from him. He asked me, "In that situation, if you told me 2 + 2 = 5, wouldn't it be okay to say you're wrong?" My response was, "Actually, when you think someone is wrong, that's the most important time to validate them!" Remember The Dress. In your reality, The Dress is blue and black (or 2 + 2 = 4), but for the other person, it's white and gold, and 2 + 2 = 5. Despite knowing the "true" color of The Dress, the people who see it as the "incorrect color" *cannot change the way they see it.* To you, 2 + 2 = 5 is wrong, but the other person may not believe that they are wrong at all!

Depending on your personal goals for the conversation, and your common goals as a team, it might be time to get curious. Take a moment to ask how they came up with their belief. Do your best to understand their logic, how they feel, and why they think the way they do. Reflect and validate what they explain. Remember that validating doesn't mean you agree with them, but it can help them feel understood. That will give space for you to then explain how *you* think and feel about 2 + 2.

Thinking 2 + 2 = 5 may be a bit of a silly example, but it is meant to show that in some situations it may take a lot of practice to get to the point where you can think and accept, "How they see it is different from how I see it, and that's okay." Remind yourself that both of your realities are equally valid; you are both human beings and both deserving of respect. Remind yourself that you think you're right, but so do they.

Anyone who expects everyone else to agree with them will wind up exhausted and frustrated. Anyone who accepts another person's perspective while still honoring their own will lead a more peaceful life. The world is full of different perspectives; accepting there are many different realities will get you far because you won't get sidetracked by defensiveness. In most cases, it doesn't matter who is "right" or "wrong"; what we need to do is understand each other so we can move on and find solutions and compromises.

THE URGE TO DEFEND YOURSELF

As I've mentioned, the urge to defend our realities is very strong. The urge to defend our version of ourselves can be even stronger. If someone thinks something about you that you feel is incorrect, you might be thinking, "When it comes to me, my reality *is* more valid. So I can defend myself because I know myself best!"

Sorry to break it to you, but this is not the case. When someone "has us wrong," it causes us major defensiveness, which doesn't always lead to us being clear or describing ourselves well. It can be excruciating to know there is someone out there in the world walking around with an "incorrect" opinion of you—just because you know you're a good person doesn't mean some people won't see your "resting bitch face" and assume you're mean. Knowing someone has an unfavorable opinion of you can be extremely uncomfortable, and it's very hard and sometimes nearly impossible to let it go. If you really want to change the mind and opinion of another person, you can speak with them, model the behavior you know you are capable of, and try to change their mind in any other way you can think of, . . . but it might just come down to , rather than defending yourself, instead giving yourself validation and getting validation from those who know you well.

So, when you are describing things about yourself, keep it tentative and don't impose "the way you know you are" as fact on another person, because they might have had a very different experience with you, and that's okay! Remind yourself that there are going to be other realities out there, that people see colors differently (The Dress), and that is something we all need to accept.

A PREMATURE END TO A CONVERSATION

There will be times that, despite your best efforts at setting a conversation up for success, you and/or the other person might not be in a place to have a productive conversation. Your conversation partner (or you) might be avoiding, switching topics, or having an intense emotional reaction. It's always an option to shut the conversation down and come back to it if and when it feels more productive. It can be tempting to shut things down if things are not going your way, but I encourage you to push through it, use your validation skills, and try your best to achieve your personal goals. If your goals cannot be met, then it may truly be time to shut down that interaction.

To do this, first acknowledge the blocked situation. Then try to set a specific time/place to try again.

* "It seems like we're a bit blocked on finding solutions. Would you be okay if we came back to this later, at [specific time/place]?"
* "I'm getting the sense we're not understanding each other here. What do you think about taking a break and trying again tomorrow evening?"

It's important to choose another time and place so that your personal goals don't get left unattended to and unresolved. You can check in about how you're both feeling about continuing the conversation at that point, or if more time is needed or your goals have changed.

During the time apart, engage in your calming-down and self-care skills to emotionally prepare for coming back to the conversation later. To logistically prepare, think about what will make the next conversation more successful. A different time of day or location? Having a therapist present to be a mediator? Recheck your goals to see if they're realistic, fair, and achievable. Come up with some solutions and compromises to suggest.

If the conversation still doesn't go as planned the next time around, it might be worth looking into a therapist or other mediator, rethinking your personal goals, or ending the relationship (see Chapter 15).

CONCLUSION

Conversations can be hard, and sometimes they don't go perfectly as planned. In this chapter, you've seen how the Ten Skills of Communication can be applied in especially tricky situations, and you're now prepared to handle even the most difficult conversations!

Chapter 14

SETTING BOUNDARIES
SKILLFULLY

INTRODUCTION

Boundary-setting is the reason I wrote this book, and possibly the reason you are reading it. I've had so many clients ask me about how to set boundaries, it is why I came up with these conversation steps in the first place! However, in order to get to the steps of boundary-setting, I first needed to lay out the foundational skills of communication that you learned in Part I. Now that you understand communication and have the ten skills under your belt, you're ready to learn how to set boundaries effectively!

WHAT ARE BOUNDARIES?

Boundaries are limits and rules in a relationship. Boundaries can fall into many categories—emotional, physical, verbal, time, sexual, material, and more. And, of course, there are different types of relationships, such as romantic, work, and family, so many kinds of potential boundaries can exist. The following table presents some examples of boundaries.

VARIOUS TYPES OF BOUNDARIES BY RELATIONSHIP TYPE

	Family	Friends	Workplace	Romantic
Emotional Boundary	I am not okay with passive-aggressive behaviors from family members. I am okay with respectful expressions of different opinions.	I'm not okay with friends taking advantage of how I feel and using it against me. I am okay with a mutual expression of emotion.	I am not okay with coworkers blaming me for things I didn't in fact do. I am okay with having honest discussions about what is working and what is not working in managing office stress.	I am not okay with my partner making themselves the victim when I bring up issues. I am okay with validating their discomfort when I bring up issues.
Physical Boundary	I am not okay with my family kissing me. I am okay with my family hugging me.	I am okay with a kiss on the cheek as a hello from friends. I'm not okay with kissing friends on the mouth.	I am not okay with coworkers hugging me. I am okay with a handshake from co-workers.	I am not okay with intense displays of affection in public. I am okay with holding hands in public.
Verbal Boundary	I am okay with saying "I love you" to my family members. I am not okay with family members commenting on my weight.	I am not okay with friends calling me names, even if it's a joke. I am okay with saying "I love you" to some close friends, but not all of them.	I am not okay with coworkers bad-mouthing other coworkers in front of me. I am okay with discussing work matters in a professional way.	I am not okay with my partner labeling me as "annoying." I am okay with my partner respectfully expressing that they are annoyed.
Time Boundary	I am okay with texting family members daily. I am not okay with family dropping in unannounced.	I am not okay with friends being perpetually late. I am okay with occasional lateness if there is good reason.	I am not okay with people lying about what time they leave work. I am okay with people asking to leave early.	I am not okay with my partner making last-minute plans. I am okay with having an agreed-upon date night every week.
Sexual Boundary	I am not okay with speaking to my family about my sex life. I am okay with watching movies with my family that contain nudity.	I am not okay with having casual sex with friends. I am okay speaking to certain friends about my sex life but expect them to keep it confidential.	I am not okay with sexual comments or advances in the workplace or with colleagues outside of the workplace. I am okay with learning about and discussing sexual harassment policies at work.	I am not okay with pushy physical advances when I've clearly said no. I am okay with consensual sex in a relationship.

	Family	Friends	Workplace	Romantic
Material Boundary	I am okay with my family members borrowing my car. I am not okay with family members leaving garbage in my car.	I am not okay with friends borrowing things and not giving them back. I am okay with friends borrowing things if they give them back.	I am not okay with lending personal things to coworkers. I am okay with lending company-owned office supplies but expect them back.	I am not okay with being expected to buy elaborate gifts. I am okay with giving small gifts on holidays and anniversaries.

SETTING BOUNDARIES: WHY IT'S IMPORTANT

When people don't have boundaries set, they lack protection from being emotionally or physically distressed, or even abused. In relationships without boundaries, people can feel over-extended, taken advantage of, shameful, guilty, resentful, and a whole slew of other negative emotions. Boundaries are extremely important in being able to reduce these distressing emotions and create more peaceful relationships.

Boundaries are also important because they provide a structure of respect and expectation in relationships. They help people feel safe and comfortable, making any relationship easier and more predictable.

Setting boundaries also helps us have closer relationships. Now, that can seem counterintuitive, but poor boundaries can show up in many ways, such as the urge to isolate. If you are unable to set a boundary and say no to people when you don't want to do something, you may end up avoiding them altogether, leaving you feeling isolated. Alternatively, you might do what people ask, even though you don't want to, and end up feeling resentful. You might then project your own lack of boundaries and resentment onto other people (feeling like you are consistently burdening them and causing them the same resentment that you feel), therefore isolating yourself. If you can set boundaries effectively, you will be able to feel closer to people and more confident in your relationships.

Boundaries are so important for building selfesteem and autonomy. By setting boundaries, you show yourself and others that you are worthy of respect and that your reality is valid!

SETTING BOUNDARIES: WHY IT'S HARD

If boundaries are so important, why do we struggle with them so much? There are many reasons why setting boundaries is difficult:

1. Lack of awareness of the need for boundaries
2. Not having the necessary skills to set boundaries effectively
3. Being inconsistent
4. Being caught off guard
5. Mental and behavioral blocks

I will address how to handle each one of these difficulties in this chapter. I'll also give you specific examples of boundary-setting in action, so you can get a good sense of what these conversations can look like. Let's get started!

SETTING BOUNDARIES: HOW TO DO IT

Now that you have a better understanding of what boundaries are, you can learn to set healthy ones. To do this, you'll use the Ten Skills of Communication you've already learned, and add in five new steps. Fifteen steps to set boundaries (and have conversations about them) may seem like a lot! But these steps will provide structure and organization, and give you confidence. Most important, the steps will set you up for consistency. When you are consistent, other people know what to expect, as far as what your boundaries are, and what will happen if your boundaries are crossed. Consistency makes upholding boundaries a lot more successful!

Below is the list of fifteen boundary-setting steps you will be learning. The new skills (and, in one case, an existing skill with a new name) are in bold.

1. **Be Aware of Boundary Needs**
2. Set Personal Goals
3. Choose a Time, Place, and Platform

4. Calm Down (Enough)

5. Remember to Listen

6. State Common Goals

7. Validate

8. Describe

9. **Set the Boundary** (the step of Find Solutions gets a new name here, because the *solution* is to *set the boundary*)

10. **Offer Alternatives**

11. **State Repercussions**

12. Offer Positive Reinforcement

13. Practice Self-Care

14. **Be Consistent**

15. **Reassess**

1. Be Aware of Boundary Needs

Now that you have seen examples of boundaries and been given a lot of reasons why they're important, I hope you have realized the need for them in some (or all) of your relationships. As you reviewed the table of boundaries across various types of relationships, I bet you realized you already have a lot of boundaries set that you weren't even aware of! Boundary-setting can happen naturally, and that is great because those situations are easy. However, you might have some relationships where there aren't natural boundaries, and these are the ones for you to turn your attention to and potentially have conversations about. Whatever the case, we all need boundaries.

Are you feeling taken advantage of? Exhausted? Violated? Insulted? These are clues to the need for boundary-setting. Think about specific relationships and then specific cycles or consistent areas of distress and discomfort. Though "negative" feelings aren't pleasant to have, they are a great communicator that change, potentially in the form of boundaries, is needed.

This first new step specific to boundary-setting, Be Aware of Boundary Needs, also serves as a reminder that *your boundaries are your responsibility*. It is up to you to determine what boundaries you need in your life. This awareness might take time to develop but is the first crucial step to setting boundaries successfully.

2. Set Personal Goals

Setting personal goals in boundary-setting is all about getting specific as to what boundary you are going to set. One of the reasons boundary-setting is difficult is because people often try to control the behavior of others (usually to get them to stop doing something). However, as we learned in Chapter 1, it is not a realistic goal to change the behaviors of others! Boundaries are not about telling other people what to do; instead, they communicate to others how you want to be treated and what *you* will do if you're not treated that way.

A personal goal for a boundary-setting conversation will most likely be to describe (with intent to be understood and motivate). Why? Because you are trying to get the other person to understand your boundary and to motivate them to respect your boundary. Just as with emotions and situations, if you are going to be describing your experience to someone else, you need to first understand what your experience is. You can't expect others to uphold your boundaries if you don't yet know what they are.

Be specific about the boundary you are setting. As with conversation goals, you don't want to overwhelm the other person and get derailed by too many topics. Articulating your boundaries in your own mind will help you to focus on one or maybe two boundaries per conversation to achieve maximum success. Specificity also helps with clarity. The more specific and clear you can be, the less likely it is that assumptions or miscommunications will arise.

One of the best ways to define specific, necessary boundaries for yourself is to ask *how it feels* when different boundaries are crossed. Are there situations or relationships in your life in which you consistently feel the same negative emotions, such as shame, guilt, fear, or resentment? As stated before, these feelings are a sign that boundaries are needed! To explore this more specifically, think about a situation in which you might need a boundary, and ask yourself the following questions:

- Who is involved?
- How did the other person behave?
- How did I behave?
- How am I feeling (physically, emotionally, spiritually)?
- What about the situation made me feel this way?
- What would I rather have happened?
- What am I okay with and what am I not okay with?

A therapist can also be very helpful in clarifying specific boundaries.

In addition, just as with conversation goals, it's important that boundary goals are realistic, fair, and achievable. Having realistic boundaries means *you* can consistently uphold them. In other words, the boundary cannot be for someone else to stop doing something or for someone else to act a certain way. It bears repeating that boundaries communicate situations where you feel distress and what your reactions to those situations will be. Below are some examples of unrealistic and realistic boundary-setting goals.

Unrealistic Boundary Goal	Realistic Boundary Goal
Get them to stop making jokes about my weight.	Explain to them that if they make jokes about my weight, I will feel very hurt and will shut down the conversation.
If they don't do the dishes, I will break up with them!	If they don't do the dishes, I will feel disappointed and might even need space from them for the rest of the evening.
They will be on time all the time or else I will leave.	If they are more than 15 minutes late, I will need to continue with my plans.

The goals in the left-hand column are unrealistic because they are either about controlling the other person, are too vague, or are creating repercussions that are impossible to adhere to. We'll look at setting realistic repercussions later in this chapter; for now, we can start thinking about setting goals in the "describe with intent to motivate" category.

It can be frustrating that you can't force another person to just respect your boundaries! However, here's a really important thing to keep in mind: the other person has just as much freedom as you do, and so the only thing you can control is your description and intentions. Once you've stated your boundaries and seen the results, you can then make informed decisions on how you will proceed.

3. Choose a Time, Place, and Platform

Where possible, the first conversation you have with someone about boundaries should not occur in the moment a boundary is crossed. This is because the person whose boundary was crossed is most likely feeling hurt/vulnerable/violated/angry, and the person who crossed it will be a lot more likely to be defensive seeing these emotions. Once you've had a boundary crossed, note it, and then plan to address it at another time using all your communication skills. Once you have had this conversation about your boundaries and have been specific about what will happen *the next time the boundary is crossed*, everyone will be on the same page. And if, later, the boundary is crossed again, you can address it in the moment.

4. Calm Down (Enough)

If someone crosses your boundary, it can be a very emotionally charged experience. Those feelings are okay and even useful. Do what you need to do, and take the time you need (if you can) to be "calm enough" to keep focused on the conversation.

5. Remember to Listen

Remind yourself of your listening skills before the conversation. Sometimes we have the urge to predict how a boundary will land before we actually give space to let the other person react.

6. State Common Goals

Start the conversation by stating common goals ("We want a good relation-ship, "We like having each other to talk to," "We both want each other to feel good," "We respect each other," etc.). This allows for positivity, aligns you both as members of the same team, and creates buy-in from the other person. As before, choose a general goal you know the other person will agree with.

7. Validate

Based on your history together, can you identify positive intentions that might have gone awry when the other person crossed your boundaries? Then use your validation skills to understand their side first. Although you might want to jump to describing, it's very important to validate first; otherwise, they'll most likely defend their intentions and their lack of aware-ness rather than hearing your side.

- "When you make jokes about me being shaped like a snowman, it seems like you're trying to have fun and make us both laugh. I don't think you mean any harm."

Again, this phase may be difficult because you have to validate someone else's reality while you are under stress. Remember: accepting and validat-ing does not mean *agreeing*. Accepting and validating that *they* think it's okay to make jokes about your weight does not mean that *you* condone it, think it's okay, or agree with it. From their perspective, they are simply making jokes, whereas you see the joking as inappropriate.

Validation models understanding so that the other person will be more likely to accept and understand your reality in the next step. Validation also ensures understanding of someone else's reality, intentions, and needs, which will be helpful in the "Offer Alternatives" step, later.

8. Describe

This is when you get to state how you feel. Use your describing skills and "I" language to show your own perspective. Be direct and concise, and use emotion words. How does it feel when the other person crosses your boundary?

- "I feel really _____ when _____."

Just as before, it's helpful to avoid the word "you." So instead of "I feel really hurt when *you* make jokes about my weight," try, "I feel really hurt when jokes *are made* about my weight." Even better, say, "I'm hurt when *I feel like* jokes are being made about my weight."

This phrasing minimizes defensiveness if the other person, in their reality, does not feel they've made jokes about your weight. What you've just made is a 100 percent factual statement across all realities.

Just as we discussed in Chapter 7 ("Describe"), when you're setting boundaries, there are times when it's helpful to be concise and times when it's okay to say more. Overexplaining your boundary and why you feel you need it can be setting up the other person to argue your reasoning and rebut each point, making it extremely difficult to actually set the boundary. In these situations, you can omit the describing step and move directly to the next step of setting the boundary. If you decide to skip describing, make sure to do self-care and get validation elsewhere! You can also leave out the describing step if the reason why you're setting the boundary is none of the other person's business! For example, if you don't want to be around people drinking because it reminds you of your ex who was drunk a lot, all people really need to know is your boundary of not wanting to be around people drinking and, potentially, that it makes you uncomfortable.

On the other hand, sometimes describing can really help someone understand your boundaries and respect them because they know more about your reality. The best way to know what to do (describe or not describe) is to think about past experiences with this person. What has happened in the past? Are they usually understanding or argumentative? If you are still unsure, err on the side of brevity, then see how things go. You can always add in more explanation later.

9. Set the Boundary

After you've described how you feel (or skipped that step), it's time to give the proposed solution to the boundary crossing, which is the boundary itself. In the Ten Skills of Communication, the eighth skill was Find Solutions. In boundary-setting, this step is Set the Boundary. It's literally a call to action for a change in behavior, and as such is one of the most important parts of boundary-setting.

This is the part of the conversation you might have been waiting for! There are ways to state boundaries that will lead to more success. Sometimes your first urge can be to say something like this:

- "You need to stop making jokes about my weight."
- "You need to stop texting me every day so I can study. It's too much!"

These are valid boundaries, but this type of phrasing will most likely not go over well because it is:

1. telling someone what to do. ("You need to stop.")
2. imposing your reality that they are making jokes about your weight or that they are currently texting too much. In their reality, they might not be doing these things.
3. taking something away from them (what they can't say or do).

Instead, frame the change you'd like to see as a chance for them to help you—giving them an opportunity rather than taking something away. If they care about you, this should be easy.

- "I'm wondering if you could help me out by trying not to comment about my physical appearance, even if the comments are well-intentioned. What do you think?"
- "Would it be okay for us to connect just once per week while I've got exams? That would really help me out."

What these are: questions, calls to action, requests to be on the same team. What these are *not:* telling them what to do, making them (or their behavior) the problem.

After setting a clear, concise boundary, let it land! This is one of the key times when your earlier reminder to yourself to *listen* will come in handy! See how they react to the boundary, and validate their reality before moving on.

10. Offer Alternatives

This is another new step for boundary-setting conversations, and an extremely important one that often gets missed. When you set a boundary with someone, the result is that you usually take something away from them that they are used to having (time, attention, subjects to talk about, physical expressions of emotions). That need is now left unmet by the new boundary, so providing an alternative can help them feel better about the change. Here's an analogy I love to use when thinking about offering alternatives:

In the Indiana Jones action movie *Raiders of the Lost Ark,* there is a famous scene where Indiana Jones is in a cave about to steal a treasure. The treasure is on a pedestal that knows the treasure's exact weight. If the treasure if taken off its resting place, traps will be set off and our hero will be killed! Indiana Jones takes a bag of sand, holds it in one hand, and feels its approximate weight. Then, he puts his other hand on the treasure, and, in one seamless, fast-as-lightning motion, he swaps out the treasure for the bag of sand. Unfortunately, he still sets off the traps, but that makes for a much better movie and—spoiler alert—he survives anyway!

How does this Indiana Jones story relate to boundary-setting? When setting boundaries, we need to be aware of replacing the now unmet need with something of equal value to the other person, so that the other person doesn't get "set off." Think about the now unmet need. What is its value or weight? What can you use as a "bag of sand" to "Indiana Jones" them and meet their needs in a different way?

Try to keep things positive. Instead of focusing on what you can't give, offering alternatives focuses on what you can give. For example:

- "I'm wondering if you could help me out by trying not to comment about my weight, even if it's well-intentioned? I'm totally fine with your other jokes about politics/what I wear/how silly my cat is."
- "Can we text once per week?" instead of "Can we stop texting once per day?"

Keeping alternatives positive by asking for what you *do* want, and not focusing on what you *don't* want, already sets you up for success. It can get the other person excited about meeting your needs and making you happy, instead of making them feel like they did something wrong and jumping into defensive mode. The weight example above touches on both the things that are unwanted and the things that are wanted. The second example, about texting, focuses only on what is wanted. You can use the combo or just focus on the positive, depending on the situation. Sometimes it's helpful to the other person to be on the same page with how things are currently, so the change is apparent: "Instead of texting every day, can we try to connect once per week?" The choice is up to you.

If the other person isn't immediately open to your boundary, that's okay! They might be caught off guard or feeling really bad. In their reality, they might not think anything is wrong (though to you it can seem *so* obvious). Validate their feelings of shock or confusion. Switch between validating and describing, trying not to impose your reality on them, until everyone feels understood and heard.

11. State Repercussions

Stating repercussions is another added step to the communication skills for boundary-setting. And just like offering alternatives, it is often missed. The point of this step is to let the other person know *beforehand* what will happen in the future if they cross the boundary you have communicated. While not always a necessary step, it can be extremely helpful in being clear about future reactions—why they happen and what they mean. Repercussions are not meant to "scare" the other person into behaving well but rather to prepare them for what's going on, and, even more important, to explain *why* you will be doing what you're doing. It lets them in on what Automatic Thoughts to have to make sense of the situation, so their own Automatic Thoughts don't run wild! Repercussions are not punishments but rather reactions to boundary-crossing behavior. Below are some helpful steps in setting repercussions:

1. Decide if a repercussion is necessary.

This depends on the situation and person. Repercussions are usually needed in cases where you feel the boundary will indeed be crossed in the future, despite your being clear on what it is. Thinking about repercussions beforehand can also hold you accountable for upholding the boundary in the future.

2. Choose a repercussion.

If you decide you need a repercussion, here's where you decide what it will be. A repercussion can be how you will feel or how you will act (or both). For example:

- "I will feel annoyed." (how you will feel)
- "I will stop the conversation and go home." (how you will act)
- "I will ignore the message." (how you will act)
- "I will feel hurt, stop the conversation, and go home." (how you will feel and how you will act)

3. Make sure it's realistic.

One of the most important parts of choosing repercussions is the same as for goal-setting: they need to be realistic! This is what delineates an empty threat from a repercussion. Empty threats often come up when we're trying to set a boundary but overshoot our repercussions in order to feel in control or elicit a response from the other person. Try to think of something that is of similar significance to the boundary being crossed. For example, it may be extreme and unrealistic to say:

- "I will never see you again if you make another comment about my weight."
- "I'll stop being friends with you if you text too often."

A more fitting repercussion might be:

- "If you make comments about my weight, I will feel extremely hurt, end the conversation, and take some time to myself because I am really upset."
- "If you text me during exam time, I'll feel frustrated and won't answer because I'm stressed and just need the time to study."

Using untrue threats, such as, "We're breaking up," "We will never talk again," or "I quit," are damaging to a relationship, as they create a culture of fear. Empty threats are also damaging in that they invalidate the things you say in the future. The most important part of choosing a repercussion is to choose one you can stick to. Otherwise, it will not be taken seriously.

To find repercussions that you think you can uphold, try the following:

- Visualize what it would look like if your boundary were crossed.
- Think about how you would feel. What would your physical and emotional reactions be?

- What would you want to do? (What would be your behavioral reaction?)
- What is the repercussion you want to have in place? Imagine carrying that out.
- What emotions come up? How could you cope with them?
- Do you think this is a realistic plan?
- What blocks or resistances come up?
- Will you be able to be consistent with this repercussion? (Think of different scenarios and if/how you can cope with them.)

For example, if you tell your ex that you will not answer their texts anymore, think about how realistic that is. Is a more time-limited "no text" period a better, more realistic alternative?

4. Explain the repercussion.

After you've told the other person what repercussion you've decided on, you can choose to let them know *why* the repercussion is in place. This is extremely helpful because, in the moment, people may interpret your boundary-crossing repercussions in ways you may not have intended! Their Automatic Thoughts might not be what you'd hoped for. Preparing the other person for repercussions and telling them the reasoning behind the repercussions will limit the chance that they'll assign their own interpretations. For example, instead of having Automatic Thoughts of "They hate me," "They're going to break up with me," or "I'm a terrible friend," they can hopefully have more realistic thoughts: "They told me if they don't respond it's because they're stressed and busy." This clear communication of intent can help sidestep many hurt feelings and miscommunications!

- "When I end the conversation, it's because I need time to myself to take care of the emotions. I still love you and want to be in a relationship, but when those comments are made, I need time to manage the hurt they cause me."

5. Get their input.

You can ask the other person if they are comfortable with the repercussion and understand what will happen and, if you choose to, why it will happen.

- "How does that seem to you?"
- "Is there anything that is unclear about what will happen?"
- "Is there anything unclear about why I feel the need to react that way in the future?"

Use your listening skills to really understand what's going on for them. Validate as needed!

12. Offer Positive Reinforcement

Let the person know what they do that you like. Thank them for helping you and listening to you. Let them know that you care about them and respect them. Thank them for respecting your boundaries.

13. Practice Self-Care

Use the self-care skills you've learned in this book (or ones you already practice) after the boundary-setting conversation.

14. Be Consistent

This is another new skill specific to boundary-setting. Now that you have chosen realistic, fair, achievable boundaries, and, potentially, repercussions, stick to the plan! Being consistent with your boundary and associated repercussions is very important in having that specific boundary and any future boundaries respected. It also lessens the confusion for the other person. For example, if you find yourself in a situation where you can't stick to the repercussion, you can address why with the other person. Maybe you are at a party and so can't leave the conversation to take time by yourself.

- "I know I mentioned that I'd leave the conversation if you made a comment about my weight, but since we're at a party, I'm going to stay. But I will need some time to myself later."
- "I know I said _____ would happen, but because of [circumstances], _____ will happen instead. What do you think?"

If you choose not to address the crossed boundary in the moment, letting the other person know at a later time that the boundary was crossed will be helpful in them remembering and respecting the repercussions of crossing it later.

In some scenarios, people may try to bait you into breaking your boundary and being inconsistent. Remember the example of the person not responding to texts from their ex? The ex might come back with a "I need help"- or "I'm lonely"-themed text to pull heartstrings and get a reply. Or they might even come back with a "You're a terrible person"-themed text to try to get you to defend yourself. These are difficult situations! Think about how you will cope with this (call a friend, turn off your phone, walk away). If you already have set up realistic repercussions and a coping plan beforehand, it's easier to stick to the plan in the moment and be consistent in upholding your boundaries and repercussions. Plan ahead for different scenarios, and you'll be able to maintain consistency!

15. Reassess

This is the final new skill associated with boundary-setting. Reassessing is important because, as stated in the beginning of this chapter, part of why boundaries are difficult is that they change! Being aware of your boundaries and addressing how they might change under different circumstances can be extremely helpful in communicating them and therefore being able to uphold them.

If boundaries change due to a change in circumstance, yet you don't communicate those boundary changes, your boundaries may seem inconsistent, which can be very confusing to others! For example, you used to be okay with texting your best friend every day, but now it's exam time and you don't have time to text daily. Unless you directly address this change with your friend, they will most likely be confused about the change in texting frequency!

Sometimes, despite our best efforts, we've chosen repercussions that were too hard to stick to. The reassessing step is also a reminder to check your consistency overall.

To reassess, think about a boundary you have set and ask yourself the following questions:

- Have my physical, emotional, time, stress-management, energy, or any other needs changed?
- Has my relationship changed?
- Have my expectations changed?
- Have other circumstances changed?
- Have I been consistent in upholding my repercussions, or do I need to choose new ones?

If you've had trouble with a specific boundary or have just set a new one, put a reminder in your calendar to mentally reassess it at a later date using the questions above.

Being consistent with boundaries requires work but is important in helping your boundaries be respected. Constantly check in on how *you* are behaving if your circumstances have changed or if the boundary has been unsuccessful. Regular conversations about changing circumstances, and therefore changing boundaries, will help both people be on the same page. Again, this takes work! However, if you put the work in, you will get all the benefits of the results.

BOUNDARY-SETTING IN ACTION

Let's see these fifteen boundary-setting skills in action! Here are some common scenarios I'm often asked about by clients: saying "no," canceling plans, managing conflicting boundaries, mediating boundaries between children, and setting physical boundaries, work boundaries, and boundaries around punctuality and space.

How to Skillfully Say No

Saying no is a boundary I get asked about often. Here is an example of how you can use the fifteen boundary-setting steps to say no to a last-minute request to help with planning a party.

1. Be Aware of Boundary Needs

The feeling in the moment that you can't, or really don't want to, do this favor for your friend. Maybe you feel pressure, discomfort, or stressed out! You are not okay with helping with this last-minute request.

2. Set Personal Goals

Your goal is to say no.

3. Choose a Time, Place, and Platform

This is easy: it's in the moment! If last-minute favors are becoming a boundary theme you want to address, you can address it in a separate conversation before the next request comes up!

4. Calm Down (Enough)

Do whatever calming exercises you may need before and during the conversation.

5. Remember to Listen

Remind yourself of how to listen well! You might feel the urge to jump in with apologizing because you assume their reaction will be negative. Listen to how they react to your boundary first, then react. They might be totally fine with you saying no!

6. State Common Goals

"We both want your party to be a success."

7. Validate

"You're really stressed about this party and need help picking up the cake."

8. Describe

"Unfortunately, I'm also swamped today. . . ." You can also choose to omit this step if you think the other person will argue your reality that you are swamped. Omitting descriptions can be extremely helpful when you're saying no, so only describe if you feel the other person needs to know or will respect your reality enough to accept it (and won't come back and argue, "You're not swamped.").

9. Set the Boundary

"Unfortunately, I can't go pick up the cake." Then see how it lands by using your listening skills. Maybe they knew it was a long shot and have a Plan B already lined up. Or maybe they're extremely upset and even seem angry with you.

10. Offer Alternatives

"I can call [other friend] to see if they can do it," or, "I am available to go tomorrow."

11. State Repercussions

In this case, repercussions aren't needed. However, they might be necessary if this last-minute favor-asking becomes a pattern. That might look something like, "Lately, I've felt pressure from some last-minute requests. My schedule is usually very tight, and so I need to receive a request at least a day in advance. Otherwise, I won't be available to pitch in."

12. Offer Positive Reinforcement

Comment on the behavior you'd like to see more of in the future. "Thank you for understanding. I really appreciate you respecting my schedule."

13. Practice Self-Care

Take a mental refreshment break to celebrate setting and upholding your boundary!

14. Be Consistent

They might keep asking, or you might just feel guilty and want to give in. Notice these urges, and work to be consistent and stick to your boundary! Remind yourself of your boundary goals and why you said no in the first place.

15. Reassess

Reassessment is usually not needed when saying no, but it can be helpful to reassess if your circumstances change or if you again feel uncomfortable. If you have set a repercussion, check in on that. Is this behavior becoming a cycle? If so, maybe you need to address this theme in another conversation.

How to Skillfully Cancel Plans

Many of my clients are managing chronic physical and/or mental health issues; one very challenging aspect of these issues is maintaining a social life. It's so difficult to plan to do things when you don't know how you're going to feel in the future. It can also be very difficult to have to cancel plans last-minute and try to explain why.

I have had personal experience with this. Years ago, while I was experiencing a flare-up of ulcerative colitis, my friends came over to try to convince me to go out. Although well-intentioned and very nice, the behavior made it extremely hard for me to keep saying no. It was especially difficult because, in my friends' reality, I didn't "look sick." Below is how I could respond if that scenario happened again:

1. Be Aware of Boundary Needs

This feeling of exhaustion came up every time I had to explain my situation to my friends. I started feeling really frustrated and noticed that this kept happening again and again. I was not okay with constantly having to explain myself and say no over and over again.

2. Set Personal Goals

The first goal that comes to mind is that I want my friends to respect my decisions and believe me when I say I'm too sick to go out! But that is not a realistic, fair, or achievable goal because it's about controlling their behavior (i.e., forcing them to respect me). Instead, my goal would be to explain the boundary that, when I need to cancel, I will do so with as much notice as possible but that I will not overexplain.

3. Choose a Time, Place, and Platform

As a pattern, it would be best to discuss flare-ups before I want to deploy the boundary. So anytime I am hanging out with one of my friends in a private, low-stress, one-on-one environment, I can take time to fully talk about the situation, and we can talk more easily about boundaries.

4. Calm Down (Enough)

I'd probably do some breathing beforehand, and having ice water on hand would help as well, because I can get worked up about this topic!

5. Remember to Listen

I would remind myself to listen and see what comes up for my friend(s). Are they curious about my autoimmune disease? Are they confused? I won't know until I give them a chance to speak.

6. State Common Goals

"We both respect each other as friends and want to support each other and spend time together when we can."

7. Validate

"I bet it can be really confusing to hear that I'm sick one day when I seemed fine the previous day, and maybe even still look totally healthy! And you seem to really be stoked to hang out and spend time together, so it's proba-bly disappointing and frustrating when I cancel at the last minute."

8. Describe

"I feel really awful when I have to cancel, because I want to hang out with you too! I always try to cancel with as much notice as possible, but some-times my symptoms change quickly." Or, "I hope you know that, when I cancel, it's not because I don't respect your time or I don't want to hang out. It's that I really don't have the energy or capacity."

Notice how this last statement helps my friend(s) get set up for inter-preting my intentions in the future rather than relying on their own Auto-matic Thoughts to make sense of the situation.

I could even add, "Is it okay to tell you a bit more about what's going on with my health?" Asking can be helpful because my friend(s) without the illness really don't have much information, and so learning a bit more can increase their buy-in. General education on the disease could be helpful for my friend(s) in satisfying their curiosity or alleviating their confusion. I can go into different levels of detail depending on who I am talking to.

9. Set the Boundary

"If I am not feeling well, I'll be canceling plans even when it's last-minute. It would really help me out if things were left at that, not because I'm mad or don't want to talk to you, but because when I'm sick I have a really hard time explaining what's going on with what little energy I have."

Then I'd use my listening skills to see how it lands. If they are really un-derstanding, the conversation might end there. Whatever their reaction is, I would, of course, validate it!

10. Offer Alternatives

"I'd be happy to make other plans after I feel better."

11. State Repercussions

Here, a small repercussion might help. "If I do need to cancel, and you push me to come out anyway or ask a lot of questions, I will politely remind you about my situation. I might also need to end the conversation so that I can focus on my recovery. How would that work for you?" Here the repercussion of just not engaging in pushy or over-questioning behavior seems like it fits well.

12. Offer Positive Reinforcement

I could close the conversation like this: "Thank you so much for talking with me about this and agreeing to try doing things a little differently. I appreciate your respect and that you're trying to understand what life with chronic illness is like."

13. Practice Self-Care

Debriefing in a journal or with another friend would be really useful for me. Since I know this is a conversation that might need to happen again, I can reflect on what went well, what I might do differently next time, and how I'd modify the conversation for different people in my life.

14. Be Consistent

Having the foresight to know that it's hard for people to change can help me prepare for the next time this situation comes up. It's important that I stick to my boundary. If I don't, it will make it harder to uphold the boundary in the future or set other types of boundaries with friends.

15. Reassess

After a few months (and after the boundary has been used), I could do a casual check-in with my friends: "How's it been going with you since we last spoke about canceling plans?"

How to Skillfully Manage Conflicting Boundaries

There will be times when you and someone else have conflicting boundaries. I see this often in my work with couples; for example, in resolving conflict, one person wants to talk things out right away, while the other person needs time to process. Here is what I often suggest as a way to compromise between these two different sets of needs:

1. Be Aware of Boundary Needs

One or both of you have noticed that you have very different needs when it comes to resolving conflict. One likes to "get it over with" and talk about it right away, whereas the other one wants space. You might not be okay with putting a conversation on hold indefinitely, or you might not be okay with not having time to collect your thoughts. You've noticed that this difference in needs often takes center stage, and the underlying issue gets ignored. Realizing that this is a frustrating cycle will help you know that boundaries are needed.

2. Set Personal Goals

The goals would likely be: Understand each other's reality, then find solutions to try.

3. Choose a Time, Place, and Platform

Once you've noticed the cycle of differences in conflict management styles, think about a time and place where you can discuss the issue on its own, not when you are in the middle of a conflict management situation!

4. Calm Down (Enough)

Do whatever you need to do to prepare for the conversation emotionally, physically, and logistically.

5. Remember to Listen

Remind yourself how to be a good listener.

6. State Common Goals

A common goal could be: "We both want to have a happy relationship where we can productively solve conflict and respect each other."

7. Validate

Depending on which type of person you are (wants to talk right away or needs time), validate the *other person's* needs. Consider why they have that need. People who want to talk things through in the moment most likely don't want issues looming and have an urge to resolve problems as quickly as possible. They might also be fearful that the conversation is going to be avoided forever or never resolved. People who need time to process usually feel anxious or overwhelmed. They need time to calm down and gather their thoughts because they might feel afraid that they'll say the wrong thing.

8. Describe

Share your reality. What goes on for you when topics emerge? What feelings come up for you?

9. Set the Boundary

Depending on what needs you have, when something is brought up, you can opt to set aside time before addressing it or ask that it be addressed within a certain time. For example, "It would really help me feel better if we could have a quick break when we have conflict, so we can reflect and then come back together after I've gathered my thoughts." Or, "If we take time for a break, I'd feel a lot more reassured if we could make specific plans to be sure to come back to the topic later." Listen to their reaction and validate it.

10. Offer Alternatives

"Depending on the situation, we can set a phone timer to take a break, then come back to the situation after thirty minutes, or we can set a specific date and time to revisit the issue." This helps both parties feel the issue will be eventually resolved, but there is time to calm down and think before discussing.

11. State Repercussions

A repercussion is probably not necessary when discussing a communication process.

12. Offer Positive Reinforcement

Thank each other for compromising and for taking time to understand each other's realities!

13. Practice Self-Care

As needed, do what you want to take care of yourself afterward. This might look like spending some quality time together to feel connected and decompress as a couple or, on the other hand, taking some time apart to process the conversation.

14. Be Consistent

Remember the plan you chose! Be consistent with setting your five-minute timer when conflicts arise, and then be sure to come back and discuss, as planned.

15. Reassess

As part of the solution, you might build in a time to review how the new communication process is working. Or after a few times of using this compromise strategy, check in with each other and see how it's going. "How is it feeling for you? What might need to change? What would you like to stay the same?"

How to Skillfully Mediate Boundary-Setting between Children

If you're a parent with more than one child, you're likely very familiar with bickering between siblings (and if you're not a parent but have siblings yourself, you can probably remember bickering with them when you were younger!). Boundary-setting can be used to mediate disputes between people—in this case, I'll use an example of one sibling borrowing another's clothes without asking and discuss how the parent can facilitate boundary-setting.

1. Be Aware of Boundary Needs

As a parent, you've noticed this argument keeps happening again and again and again. . . . Everyone is fed up with the cycle, and one of the siblings is really not okay with the other one borrowing their clothes.

2. Set Personal Goals

The goal here is to understand both children's realities and come up with firm boundaries and known repercussions.

3. Choose a Time, Place, and Platform

Pick a moment when the siblings are not worked up. If the argument has just happened, you can ask them to go calm themselves first, and they can even start brainstorming solutions to bring when you discuss solutions later.

4. Calm Down (Enough)

For a mediator, things can get frustrating! If you can stay calm, the chances of your kids staying calm are a lot higher. Do what you need to in order to prepare mentally, physically, emotionally, and logistically. Help the kids calm down if they need it (you can teach them the breathing exercises from this book).

5. Remember to Listen

Remind your kids that only one person talks at a time. Use a "talking item" if you need to; only the person holding the item gets to talk. Remind yourself to really listen to the kids too! Sometimes their thoughts and feelings get easily overlooked just because they're kids. Taking the time to listen to them can be extremely powerful and helpful.

6. State Common Goals

For example, try, "We all want to live peacefully together and feel respected," and check the response to ensure buy-in from both parties.

7. Validate:

Take turns showing understanding for both parties. Sibling 1, for instance, gets extremely frustrated when their clothes are borrowed without them being asked first. They feel disrespected and unheard. This makes them feel very angry! Sibling 2 gets confused by this anger because they always return things, and Sibling 1 "wasn't using it anyway." They are also confused because they are fine with sharing their own clothes. Modeling this understanding of each side and taking time to really understand both siblings can be very helpful. Doing this helps them see that there is one situation yet two very different interpretations (just like The Dress). No one is "right," and no one is "wrong." Underscore that both interpretations and all associated emotions are valid but that a solution is still needed.

8. Describe

It's not required that you bring in your own reality, but if you want, you can say how it hurts you that the siblings can't get along or that you feel frustrated when there is yelling going on in the house over borrowed clothes. If you do this, you'll be modeling for your children how to express emotions.

If you feel like describing will derail the conversation, though, you can skip it. Most likely it is not needed in a case like this, as you have already facilitated the describe step by validating both siblings' realities while they listened to each other.

9. Set the Boundary

"Going forward, Sibling 2 will not borrow Sibling 1's clothes without asking, and vice versa!" Notice how *the boundary goes both ways*, even though there is only one sibling who had negative feelings around borrowing without asking. Listen to their reactions, and validate them as needed so that they both feel understood before moving on.

10. Offer Alternatives

To borrow something, each person must ask first and then set an agreed-upon time to give it back (one week, one day, etc.). Again, the rules apply to both siblings.

11. State Repercussions

Due to the disagreement and heated feelings, repercussions might be needed. If someone borrows something without asking, for example, they must pay the other sibling ten dollars or one dollar or a penny, or some other agreed-upon repercussion. Making the sibling who borrowed without asking do chores might not be a great repercussion, as it does not benefit the sibling who was borrowed from without asking. Ask for input from both children as to what would be fair, then use your listening skills, validate the needs behind their responses, and agree upon the repercussions.

12. Offer Positive Reinforcement

Thank the siblings for working to understand each other's feelings around this issue and coming to a compromise together.

13. Practice Self-Care

You might want some alone time after this conversation. The siblings also might need some help being directed toward activities that will help them process their emotions.

14. Be Consistent

As the mediator, make sure to honor the boundaries and repercussions by remembering and following through on what both children agreed to.

15. Reassess

Check in with the siblings and see how it's going. Does anything need to be changed? What is working well?

How to Skillfully Set Boundaries around Punctuality

This is another common issue, and also one that's come up for me personally. In my case, I lived near a friend—I'll call her Sam—who didn't have her driver's license. She often asked me for rides. At first, I didn't mind, especially if we were going to (or near) the same place. But then I started noticing Sam was *always* late, and I'd be waiting for her for fifteen or twenty minutes. I felt extremely disrespected, frustrated, and unappreciated. After all, I was the one doing her a favor! Here's how I handled the situation:

1. Be Aware of Boundary Needs

I noticed that this was happening repeatedly. I was spending a lot of time sitting in my car waiting for Sam, and I was not okay with that! I was starting to feel resentful toward her, which was damaging to our relationship as a whole. These repetitive cycles and negative feelings were my signs that something needed to change.

2. Set Personal Goals

"To set a boundary with my expectations of what will happen if she's late" (describe with intent to motivate and be understood).

3. Choose a Time, Place, and Platform

I chose to have this conversation one day when Sam and I were hanging out by ourselves. The mood was light, and we had some privacy.

4. Calm Down (Enough)

I did some simple breathing exercises beforehand. I figured that would be enough, as even though her lateness made me angry, it wasn't a very emotional issue.

5. Remember to Listen

I mentally reviewed my listening skills and reminded myself to listen respectfully throughout the conversation.

6. State Common Goals

I said to Sam, "We both respect each other and value our friendship."

7. Validate

Then I told her, "When I'm waiting for you, I believe you're trying really hard to be on time." (Notice I didn't make a "You're late" imposition, or a "You just don't see it's disrespectful" accusation—though those are urges I definitely had!)

8. Describe

I said, "When I make time to pick you up and then have to wait, I feel really frustrated and disrespected, and often I get stressed out that we'll both be late." I kept it simple and concise, not bringing up details about specific times Sam was late but rather sticking to a general theme. The past didn't matter here if I wanted to keep us focused on future scenarios.

9. Set the Boundary

"Next time we schedule a ride, I will wait for ten minutes. If you're not in the car by then, I'll leave." Notice the specific time period—ten minutes. Not just, "I'll wait a while and then leave." Then I would listen to her reaction and validate it.

10. Offer Alternatives

"If I miss you, then you can call a ride service, take the bus, or get a cab. Perhaps we can meet up later."

11. State Repercussions

In this situation, I'd already stated the repercussion—that I would leave after ten minutes. This was a very realistic, fair, and achievable repercussion. I could have chosen to ask for Sam's input, but, in this case, I didn't because I felt she might try to convince me to not have the boundary.

12. Offer Positive Reinforcement

After the conversation, I thanked Sam for understanding, respecting my boundaries, and helping me not feel so frustrated.

13. Practice Self-Care

I didn't need much self-care after this because I felt good, but I gave myself credit for finally addressing an issue that had gone on for a long time!

14. Be Consistent

The next time I went to pick Sam up, I made sure we had a set, specific time for my arrival. I showed up as scheduled and set an alarm on my phone for ten minutes. She managed to be on time!

15. Reassess

I moved out of town soon after the discussion, so there was no need to reassess the boundary—I didn't need it anymore.

How to Skillfully Ask for Space

Going away to college means keeping up with long-distance friendships, and often that means texting nonstop, which is an awesome way to keep in touch—but not so awesome in the middle of exams. If this situation applies to you, you might need to set a boundary. This is also an example of how a boundary can change when circumstances change. If your friends aren't able to limit calls or texts during your busy periods, you need to let them know you won't be as available as you were before. I touched on this scenario earlier in the book, but here is the fleshed-out version of what this boundary-setting conversation might look like.

1. Be Aware of Boundary Needs

Here you can be alerted to the fact that your circumstances have changed; you have less time for friend communication during exams, so you're no longer okay with texting daily. However, if you didn't catch that, your new reaction of feeling frustrated with messages from your friend when the messages used to elicit joy would be a hint that a new boundary is needed.

2. Set Personal Goals

To let the friend know you can't message as much for the next month (describe with intent to be understood).

3. Choose a Time, Place, and Platform

During the next call, text, email, or face-to-face interaction, depending on the complexity of the circumstances and the relationship.

4. Calm Down (Enough)

Any option, as needed!

5. Remember to Listen

Refresh your memory about good listening skills before going into the conversation. This is important in order to be able to understand how the boundary is received in their reality so you can then validate and respond accordingly.

6. State Common Goals

"We both value the relationship. We want to stay in touch as much as possible; we care about what's going on in each other's lives."

7. Validate

"You seem to have a lot going on and are probably used to texting every day to check in and feel connected."

8. Describe

"I'm getting stretched really thin right now and am stressed about exams and studying."

9. Set the Boundary

"I'd love it if we could continue to text, though, maybe once per week for the next month while I finish exams." Listen to their reaction and validate it.

10. Offer Alternatives

"Or, instead of texting, what do you think about having a phone call to make sure we fully catch up each weekend?"

11. State Repercussions

"If you need to text during the week, please know I might not answer right away. That's not because I'm mad at you or don't *want* to talk; it's only because I'm busy and stressed with studying and need to keep my focus on my schoolwork. How does that seem to you?" Notice that this repercussion involves explaining how and why the repercussion will take place. It clearly explains that not replying doesn't mean you're mad or ignoring them. This repercussion is realistic and also asks for input from the friend.

12. Offer Positive Reinforcement

"Thank you so much for understanding. Your support while I'm at school means so much to me!"

13. Practice Self-Care

As needed.

14. Be Consistent

If you receive a text, uphold the boundary. If you reply right away, this will render the boundary ineffective and possibly make it harder for your friend to respect future boundaries.

What if there is a friend emergency, and you need to break your own boundary? Imagine your friend texts you that they just went through a terrible breakup and would really like to talk. You can address that before or after you call them to provide comfort.

"I know I said we couldn't talk during the week, but because of your breakup, I of course want to put aside an hour to talk about it today! Then we can also have our regular call on the weekend to check back in. What do you think?"

A statement like this acknowledges the inconsistency in the boundary and explains that it's due to extenuating circumstances. It also reminds the other person that the boundary will be put back in place and they can expect to talk to you next on the weekend.

15. Reassess

After exams, see how you feel. Maybe you like this frequency of communication better and want to keep it up, or maybe you want to let your friend know you're available to go back to daily messaging. Check in about this with your friend using the skills from this book to structure the conversation.

How to Skillfully Stand Up for Yourself at Work

When I was first starting out as a biologist, I had many jobs. I'd work for free or for very little pay, and I'd work *hard*. I was so determined to get into that career and work my way up that I humbly put myself at the bottom and would say yes to anything and everything people asked me to do. I spent a lot of time cleaning buckets and fish tanks. After seeing my go-getter energy and "yes to everything" attitude, a couple of the more senior colleagues asked me to help them. "Of course!" I said, and then I worked faster and stayed later just to make sure everything got done. This kept happening, and I'd accept more and more responsibility, until, one day, I realized I was doing the job of about three people, and the others were not doing much at all.

I had been so wrapped up in proving myself, being well-liked, and making it in this career that I hadn't even realized I was being taken advantage of. This was a tough position to be in; it's a lot easier to start with boundaries than to retroactively put them in place. But I knew what I needed to do because I was getting very burned out! So I decided to start saying no. But it was tough—I wish I'd had these communication skills way back then. Here is an example of what I would do and say if this scenario happened to me today:

1. Be Aware of Boundary Needs

The awareness that I was doing more than my fair share was a good sign of boundaries needed, as was the resentment I was starting to feel toward coworkers and the fact that I was getting extremely burned out, both physically and mentally, from all the work I was doing! An increase in physiotherapy and chiropractic bills was an even more tangible hint that something needed to change.

2. Set Personal Goals

Only taking on what I can. Saying no to things that aren't my direct responsibility or in my job description.

3. Choose a Time, Place, and Platform

A simple no in the moment when they ask. If it becomes a bigger issue, I will have a preemptive conversation out of the moment, but this doesn't feel necessary yet.

4. Calm Down (Enough)

Doing some awareness and breathing at work will help me stay calm. Preparing for saying no before I'm asked to do something will also be helpful in feeling more calm and prepared for the conversation.

5. Remember to Listen

I will review all the listening skills I've learned and remember to allow the other person space to react so I can properly validate their reaction.

6. State Common Goals

"We all want work to go as smoothly as possible and have the animals properly taken care of."

7. Validate

"You seem really busy and overwhelmed with your daily tasks."

8. Describe

"I also feel overwhelmed and stressed sometimes by all the work to be done."

9. Set the Boundary

"To keep the animals healthy, I need to focus on my tasks, and so I can't do this extra work."

When saying no, it can be hard or impossible to frame things positively. I feel this phrasing is the best way for me to be as positive as possible. Listen to their reaction and validate it.

10. Offer Alternatives

"What I can do is keep helping with the things I'm already doing and maybe go with you to meet with our boss to talk about how we're both feeling over-extended." Or, "Have you asked [other coworker] to see if they can help you out?"

11. State Repercussions

In this case, a repercussion is not necessary.

12. Offer Positive Reinforcement

"Thanks so much for understanding."

13. Practice Self-Care

As needed.

14. Be Consistent

If they ask again, I will say no again!

15. Reassess

After a few weeks of saying no, I'll ask myself, "Am I being consistent? What might change?" And I'll think about what might happen if my duties or hours at work changed and how that could affect the boundary.

How to Skillfully Set Physical Boundaries

Physical boundaries are extremely important in any relationship. Whether we struggle with the aunt who leaves lipstick on our cheek or the coworker who ends every joke with a punch in the arm, we all have different levels of comfort when it comes to being touched and sometimes need to express how an action makes us feel. This can, of course, be complicated by situational factors and settings. For the next example, imagine you're someone who doesn't like being hugged, and you're speaking to your friend about creating a boundary. Feel free to adapt the scenario as necessary to set the physical boundaries you need with friends and family.

1. Be Aware of Boundary Needs

Think about the feeling of discomfort, both physical and emotional, that comes up when hugging other people and the realization that you are not okay with hugging friends all the time and that life would be a lot better if you could communicate that boundary!

2. Set Personal Goals

This one can seem tough because you are telling them you don't like being hugged; however, a hug is two-sided! So, for this first conversation, you can still say that you won't be participating, rather than "telling them to stop."

3. Choose a Time, Place, and Platform

Select a time and place you feel you will have privacy and time enough to discuss the topic. Try not to do this in front of other people, as the person you're talking to may feel embarrassed.

4. Calm Down (Enough)

As needed.

5. Remember to Listen

Refer back to Chapters 4 and 6 if need be. Have your listening and validation skills ready!

6. State Common Goals

"We both respect each other as friends."

7. Validate

"You hug because you are showing, affection and you probably want other people to feel good as well."

8. Describe

"However, hugging makes me feel very uncomfortable."

9. Set the Boundary and 10. Offer Alternatives

"Instead of hugging, I was wondering if we can high-five instead. That would really help me feel a lot more comfortable!" Listen to their response!

11. State Repercussions

"I'd really appreciate your help with trying this new greeting, but we might forget! So, if you do try to hug me, I'll just say 'high five' as a reminder. How does that sound?"

12. Offer Positive Reinforcement

"Thank you so much for helping me out with this and trying something new."

13. Practice Self-Care

As needed.

14. Be Consistent

Do your best to remember the new boundaries and uphold them anytime you greet each other.

15. Reassess

Check in with your friend after a while and see how they're feeling. Are you being consistent with the high fives? Do you want to try a different way of greeting instead?

PRACTICE MAKES ~~PERFECT~~ EASIER

In addition to the blocks and resistances I've addressed in this chapter, another thing that is difficult about setting boundaries is that boundary-crossing situations often catch us off guard. (Ever been surprised by a request you felt you couldn't say no to? I know I have!) To feel more prepared for spur-of-the-moment requests, it can be helpful to practice scenarios before they come up.

Think of a boundary you want to set or a boundary you wish you had set in the past. Using the Boundary-Setting Checklists in the Appendix (pages 267–269), go through each step and play out how the conversation might look. What urges do you notice coming up that might derail the conversation? What emotions might you feel? How could you cope with those emotions? What do you imagine the other person's reaction to be, and how could you handle it using the skills in this book? What might make it tough to stick to any repercussions?

If you want to take it a step further, role-play with another person. Play yourself first, then switch roles to see what it's like to be on the receiving end of your boundary. What does it feel like? What might be going on in your reality as the receiver?

If saying no is hard for you, practice by saying no to small things, even if you *can* do them. It's just practice and will not cause anyone harm (for example, a friend asking, "Can you go get me a coffee?"). More important, practicing will reduce your guilty feelings about taking this action and help you feel more confident when stakes are higher in the future. This is like exposure therapy, where you expose yourself to the thing that you are afraid of in order to desensitize the fear you have about it.

Mental and Behavioral Blocks to Setting Boundaries

In this section, I'll break down the most commons boundary-setting blocks I see, using the CBT cognitive model we discussed back in the Introduction (see page 3 for a refresher). This will help with understanding the link between your thoughts about a situation and the behavioral reactions that result from those thoughts.

1. Avoiding Setting Boundaries Out of Fear and Guilt

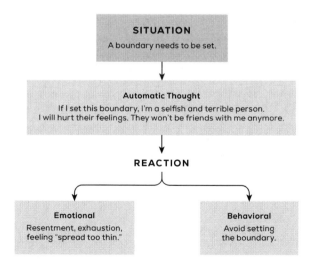

Setting boundaries can be scary! You might be scared you'll hurt someone's feelings or come across as selfish. These feelings are valid, as we don't want to cause more hurt or damage relationships, but how true are these Automatic Thoughts, really?

Presenting your boundaries, explaining them, and being respectful might still cause discomfort to the other person, but *you know you can move past it.* You now have the skills so that you can minimize their hurt by coming up with solutions together and giving them lots of positive reinforcement and validation through the boundary-setting process.

Here's a more successful version:

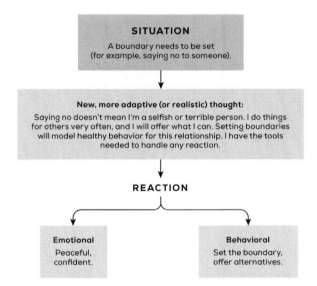

2. Avoiding Setting Boundaries Because You Don't Think You're Worth It

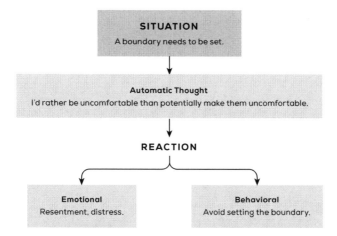

Often guilt and/or low self-esteem are underneath the consistent urge to ignore your boundaries. This is a "stuck between a rock and a hard place" type of situation. You either feel bad because your boundaries are crossed or you feel bad for setting them. Consider working with a therapist to create confidence in your value without having to overextend yourself. Remind yourself you deserve to have healthy, respectful relationships where your (realistic and fair) boundaries are respected. Then you'll be able to take part in a scenario more like this one:

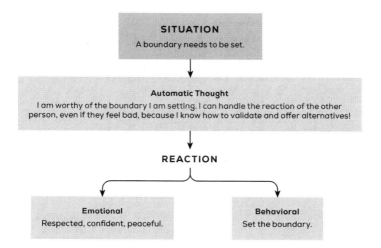

3. Having the Urge to Over-Apologize or Overexplain

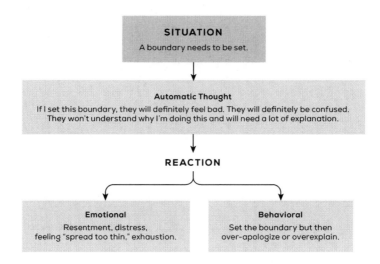

Sometimes, when we set a boundary, we feel a need to apologize or explain . . . a lot. This works against successful boundaries in that you often feel pressured to give in to your own guilt about setting the boundary. The other person can also see how unsure of your own boundary you are and will be less likely to respect it.

If you are an over-apologizer or overexplainer, ask yourself, what is the purpose? What Automatic Thoughts are coming up that are causing these reactions? Are those thoughts true?

Overexplaining or over-apologizing happens when you really want to make sure the person on the receiving end of your boundary clearly knows your intentions. If you can give "good enough reasons" or show extreme remorse, then the other person won't think you're "terrible/selfish/bad."

To manage these urges, I suggest that you set the boundary and see how the other person reacts before launching into a huge explanation or apology. Use the listening skills from Chapter 4. Remind yourself that you shouldn't assume someone's reaction. They might be fine with the boundary, or they might even be relieved! (Haven't we all been relieved when someone's canceled plans with us and we can stay at home in our pajamas?) So, first, let the boundary land and see how it's received, rather than launching into a pre-emptive defense strategy. If you're unclear how they feel after hearing the boundary, ask.

My sister and her husband do something similar with their toddler, who's recently learned to walk and is still a little unsteady on her feet. If she falls down, they don't immediately rush to her side and say, "Are you okay? Don't cry! It's okay!" They first *wait and let her decide how she feels.* If she is hurt, they of course go to comfort her, but most of the time she just gets right back up as if nothing happened! In those cases, not only would the comforting be unnecessary, it might actually prompt her to start crying!

Overexplaining and over-apologizing do the same thing; they can indirectly tell the other person that your boundary is hurtful to them because you need to apologize for it or explain it so much.

If there *is* a negative reaction, instead of giving in to your urges to over-apologize and overexplain, listen and *validate!* This is a more direct way of assuaging your guilt for setting the boundary, because you are attending to them, rather than to yourself and your own reality. Show the other person that you understand their reality and know they might be in a tough position due to your boundary. Give alternatives and work together to find solutions.

Of course, within this new framework, you can apologize if the situation calls for it. However, I encourage clients to apologize at maximum *one time* during a boundary-setting conversation. One apology is great because it shows remorse for the potential distress, inconvenience, or change you may be causing but doesn't make the other person feel like you "should" apologize a million times because you've done something "wrong."

Here's the same scenario, with the overexplaining and over-apologizing urges removed:

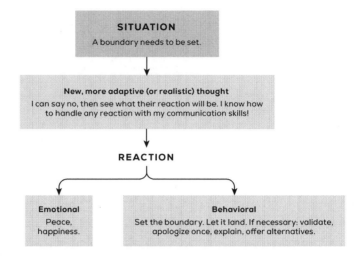

4. Avoiding Setting Boundaries Because "They Should Just Know"

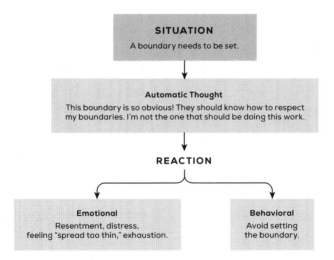

It might seem extremely obvious to us what to do or not do: say "please" and "thank you," be on time, don't be mean, and other kindergarten rules. These things feel *so obvious* to you, and are very valid, but to other people they are not as obvious. Just like our perceptions of color in The Dress, we need to describe our reality clearly so that people understand if and how it's different from their own.

Making sure we don't assume people know our boundaries takes effort, which is another reason boundary-setting can be difficult. First, you need to be very clear with yourself about what your boundaries are, which takes time and insight. Think about the distressing emotions and cycles of conflict that are signs you need some boundaries. Next comes expressing your boundaries to others, which can be scary because it puts you in a vulnerable place and poses potential changes to relationships. Being aware of these reasons for not setting boundaries or assuming that the other person will "just know" what to do or not do can motivate us to express our boundaries.

It can be really frustrating to do the heavy lifting when setting boundaries when it's the other person who is crossing them. It can seem unfair! Although some people might understand your boundaries better, and it comes naturally to them to respect them, other people don't. In those relationships, think about your common goals. Are those goals worth the heavy lifting of communicating? It can be hard to own your part in your boundaries and do the work, but it will become easier with time, and the rewards will help motivate you to keep it up! As I've said before, *your boundaries are your responsibility.*

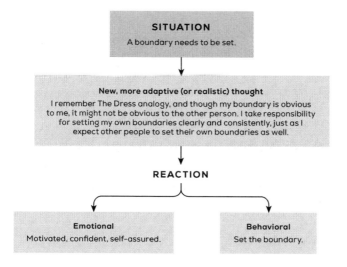

INDIRECTLY SETTING BOUNDARIES

The fifteen steps to setting boundaries make up a framework. As you grow more comfortable with boundary-setting, you will be able to adapt the steps of the framework to best fit your situation. If you are conversing with someone who is extremely difficult, pushy, or argumentative, then you may want to consider setting boundaries *indirectly*. Indirectly setting boundaries means not having a formal conversation about the boundary but rather implementing the boundary without direct communication that it's happening. This may seem very tempting to do all the time, as it allows you to avoid potentially uncomfortable conversations! It may seem contradictory to the previous statements in this chapter about the importance of being clear about boundaries. This is yet another reason why boundary-setting is difficult! I do suggest having direct conversations if you can, but there will be some rare cases where indirect boundary-setting might be a better way to go. Here are pros and cons for both direct and indirect boundary-setting:

Direct boundary-setting is:

- great for when you want to be clear about the intentions behind your actions. It may be that you really care about the other person's interpretation of your behavior and want to make it clear w*hy* you're acting the way you are. Direct boundary-setting is especially needed if the other person involved is prone to jumping to negative conclusions (e.g., taking time is interpreted as your being angry).
- great for being clear on a relationship shift.
- great for being clear on relationship expectations.
- not so good if the other person is prone to arguing your boundaries.

Indirect boundary-setting is:

* great if you aren't as invested in how your behavior comes across—the boundary is more for you and you don't care if they interpret your behaviour as rude, selfish, or otherwise negative.
* great if you've tried direct boundary-setting with a specific person, but they just argued and argued against your reasoning.
* not so good if you are just avoiding difficult boundary-setting conversations! (It's very important to realize if this is the case for you.)

As you can see, the choice between direct versus indirect boundaries depends on the type of relationship at play. When you're starting out with boundary-setting, I urge you to directly set the boundaries, as this provides much more clarity around expectations for both people involved. It also limits assumptions, avoids confusion, and gives you more practice managing difficult conversations. However, just like the boundaries themselves, the way you deliver a boundary (directly or indirectly) may need to change. This can be because a relationship might change or your boundary needs might change.

How to Indirectly Set Boundaries

Most of the steps for indirectly setting boundaries are the same as directly setting boundaries. (Sorry, but you're not getting out of doing the work just because you're setting boundaries indirectly!) A good rule of thumb is that you're just leaving out the direct communication with the other person.

1. Set Personal Goals

Be clear with yourself on what your boundaries are and what you hope to achieve. Are the goals fair, realistic, and achievable?

2. Calm Down (Enough)

Practice calming exercises during situations where boundaries are crossed so you'll be able to calm yourself when you need to indirectly set boundaries.

3. Offer Alternatives (optional)

If it'd be helpful for you to come up with an alternative, you can, but it's not necessary.

4. State Repercussions (optional)

Be clear with yourself what the repercussion will be (so you're not acting on in-the-moment impulses if the boundary is crossed). *You* get to decide if you're going to express the repercussion to the other person! But you need to be clear with yourself on how you will act, so you can be consistent.

5. Be Consistent

This is especially important in indirect boundary-setting, as you are letting your actions do the talking for you.

6. Offer Positive Reinforcement (optional)

If the other person has respected the boundary, or done something else well in the situation, be sure to point it out.

For example, "I noticed that you've stopped making comments about my weight and I really appreciate it." (You may have noticed this behavior shift after you indirectly set the boundary and repercussion that you would not "fake laugh" at those jokes anymore and would instead remain neutral and change the subject.)

7. Practice Self-Care

As needed. There might be difficult moments in maintaining indirect-boundary repercussions. Give yourself credit for your consistency!

8. Reassess

How is the indirect boundary being reacted to? Do you need to change anything? Is a different repercussion needed? Most important, do you feel a direct conversation will help the boundary be more successful?

The example scenarios I've given in this chapter have all used direct boundary-setting to give you a better sense of all the skills and to encourage you to have direct conversations when you can. I don't want to condone avoiding difficult conversations. Be honest with yourself about which type of boundary-setting, direct or indirect, is best for you and the situation, and most respectful to the other person.

RESPECTING OTHER PEOPLE'S BOUNDARIES

If we want to have our boundaries respected, we need to check that the respect is going both ways. This is a reminder that when others present boundaries, you must do your best to remain open and non-argumentative. You might not understand or agree with someone's boundary; you may think it's silly or unfair. Remember The Dress, and respect that the boundary exists even if you don't think it "should" or is necessary. If needed, use your solution-finding skills to come up with compromises.

> PRACTICE MAKES ~~PERFECT~~ EASIER

Think of a specific person in your life. What are their boundaries (physical, time, emotional, etc.) with regards to your relationship? How do they act, or what do they do or say, when their boundaries are crossed? Have they ever tried to set boundaries with you directly or indirectly? Asking these difficult questions can be extremely helpful in knowing what it's like to be on the receiving end of boundaries—and therefore will help you in setting your own boundaries!

CONCLUSION

In this chapter, I've shown you ways to manage all the reasons why boundary-setting is difficult and sometimes avoided:

1. Lack of awareness for the need of boundaries → Checking in for consistent distressing cycles and feelings in relationships.

2. Not having the necessary skills to set boundaries effectively → Fifteen steps to structure boundary-setting conversations or set boundaries indirectly without formal conversation.

3. Being inconsistent → Four specific steps in the fifteen-step boundary-setting framework address setting yourself up for consistency: Set Personal Goals, State Repercussions, Be Consistent, and Reassess.

4. Being caught off guard → Learning boundary-setting steps and practicing them consistently to feel confident when situations come up sporadically.

5. Mental and behavioral blocks → Using the CBT skills to challenge thoughts that cause these blocks, and replacing untrue Automatic Thoughts with truer, more adaptive/realistic thinking.

We all have a right to express how we prefer to be treated in our relationships. The key point to remember about boundaries is that they describe *your* actions when those lines are crossed. Ultimately, it's your responsibility to apply the skills of communication and to be consistent. You will then feel the positive effects of knowing your own boundaries and effectively communicating them to others!

Chapter 15

ENDING RELATIONSHIPS SKILLFULLY

INTRODUCTION

We've all experienced the end of a relationship. It might have been a mutual breakup, a drift apart, or a huge blowout. Ending relationships gets a bad rap, probably because it can be a painful, uncertain, and confusing process. However, sometimes ending a relationship is very necessary and, despite short-term discomfort, can lead to long-term benefits. In this chapter, I'll offer some guidance on how to figure out when ending a relationship is appropriate and how to apply the communication skills you've learned to the process. I'll also present personal stories of times when I successfully ended relationships.

ENDING RELATIONSHIPS: WHY IT'S IMPORTANT

If a relationship is causing of stress and pain, or is otherwise damaging your mental, emotional, physical, or spiritual health, it is important to know when it's time to end the relationship so that you can be healthier and happier. However, knowing *when* to let go of people and relationships is difficult. Deciding to stop communication can be very scary, whether it's with colleagues, friends, or even family members, because it leads to change in your life that you might not feel able to fully predict or feel confident coping with.

Sometimes you might want to just tell someone to f$@! off (which, of course, I can't stop you from doing). However, if you are able, I encourage you to use the Ten Skills of Communication for a more peaceful ending.

ENDING RELATIONSHIPS: WHEN TO DO IT

Deciding if and when to end a relationship is very personal. Relationships are complicated, so only you can know when it's the right time to end one. The topic of ending relationships could fill a whole other book, but I wanted to touch on this topic, even if briefly, as a reminder that it is an option for you. Sometimes, all the communication in the world can't work enough magic. Here are some situations that may warrant ending a relationship:

1. Your safety is threatened.

Being in an abusive relationship is complicated. From the outside, it can seem like a simple solution to leave; however, I've seen that is rarely, if ever, the case. Abuse sometimes starts slowly, leaving one or both people in the relationship feeling like the frog put in a pot of water that is slowly heated to a boil, so slowly that the frog does not try to jump out until it's too late. Despite the complexity, if safety is an issue, then a change needs to be made. If your safety (physical or emotional) is being threatened, speak to a therapist, friend, or crisis line, and take the first steps toward making a change.

2. You don't share common goals.

If you have no common goals, this likely means you have no common values either, and that's an issue for any type of relationship. If you're in a relationship with someone who doesn't want what's best for you or won't compromise, then you might not want to continue the relationship. Dig deep and ask yourself if it's regular, surface things you disagree about or if it is something more. Arguments and disagreements are normal! But deep underlying differences in values and goals could point to a doomed relationship. Is there anything you both value? What are the things you're both working toward?

3. The other person is unwilling to accept your reality.

As we know, disagreeing about realities is common. But a refusal to accept your experience shows that the other person has no *desire* to understand you. Sometimes, as much as the skills in this book can set you up for success, a victim mentality, bullying, defensiveness, or stubbornness will win out. Is ignoring or invalidating your reality the way someone who really cares about your best interests would treat you? How do you feel when you are around this person?

4. You are unwilling to accept their reality.

Your own unwillingness to accept someone else's reality points to your lack of respect for the relationship. Do you value this person? Do you value the common goals enough to make compromises, work on communication, set your ego aside, and work to understand their reality? If you are unwilling or unable to accept their reality, you won't be able to find solutions as a team and make reasonable compromises. No one expects you to love and respect everyone! If someone's reality is unacceptable to you, maybe you'd be better off without this person and this relationship.

ENDING RELATIONSHIPS: HOW TO DO IT

1. Set Personal Goals

To end the relationship (describe). Really check that this is the goal you want. Does the relationship need to end, or does it just require better boundaries?

2. Choose a Time, Place, and Platform

This can mean a general timeline, like having a good coping plan in place to manage the changes that will result from ending this relationship. Also think about the time and place to declare the split, especially if safety is an issue.

3. Calm Down (Enough)

Prepare for the conversation and get to a calm mental and emotional state as much as you can.

4. Remember to Listen

Remember to listen to how the other person reacts before jumping in with explanations.

5. State Common Goals (optional)

This might not be needed (or possible if you have none in common!), but it can be a peaceful way to end or to modify a relationship if you still respect the other person. If you do state common goals, focus on those that you still share, saying something like:

- "We both respect each other and want each other to be happy."
- "We both want what's best for the company."
- "We both want what's best for our kids."

Only state common goals if they are true. If you are ending the relationship because you don't have any common goals, then skip this step!

6. Describe

Because new information is being shared, this is one of the rare situations where the describing step comes before the validating step. This is an important time to be clear and concise. Just as with boundary-setting, you don't necessarily need to justify *why* you're ending the relationship if you think your reasoning will be challenged.

- "I am ending this relationship."
- "This relationship is not something I want to put time and energy into anymore."

Or use explanations (keeping them concise!):

- "I am ending this relationship because I have been consistently feeling really terrible and hurt."
- "This relationship is not something I want to put time and energy into because I want to focus more on my career and other relationships."

When describing, be sure to check you're not tempted to use the "giving bad news" or "stating intentions" urges discussed earlier in the book (see pages 95–96).

7. Validate (optional)

Again, this is a judgment call as to whether it's necessary. Feel free to validate the other person's shock, hurt, disappointment, or confusion. Or move on to the next step. The goal is to make the ending as healthy as possible for you.

8. Find Solutions (optional)

This is another step that might not be relevant—or it might be extremely necessary. Do you have lives that are intertwined? Mutual friends, living arrangements, a workplace, pets, or children? And who will get the Netflix password?!? This is something you can prepare for beforehand so you are ready with realistic suggestions and fair compromises to get the ball rolling.

9. Offer Positive Reinforcement (optional)

If you need to keep in contact with this person and will see them again, it might be worth noting their maturity or their respect for your decision. At the very least, you can thank them for listening; however, this step is not always necessary.

10. Practice Self-Care (very important!)

Ending relationships is difficult, even when it's by choice, and can leave us feeling we've been left with a hole in our lives. Therefore, be prepared with new alternatives to fill the gap. What needs will now have to be met in a different way? Answering this question is a part of your self-care plan, along with anything else you feel is necessary. Some examples include: finding a new job/career path before quitting, thinking before a breakup about how you'll spend your time and receive emotional support afterward, or considering how you will spend holidays if you aren't in touch with family members.

Self-care might involve grieving the experience or the life you *thought* you were going to have but didn't. A therapist can be very helpful in managing the emotions that come up in the grieving process.

RELATIONSHIP-ENDING SKILLS IN ACTION

Now that you've learned how to use the Ten Skills of Communication to end relationships, I will share some stories from my life where I said goodbye to an invalidating partner, a bullying coworker, and a pushy friend.

Ending a Relationship with a Partner

I had been dating a guy—I'll call him Jeremy—for about three months, and my birthday was coming up. Since we'd only been dating for a short time, I'm not super keen on birthday celebrations in general, and my birthday was on a Tuesday, I wasn't expecting anything from Jeremy. I was going to make plans to hang out with friends, but he told me to keep my schedule clear to hang out with him. Then, on my birthday, he canceled because he had to work late. I was disappointed.

I became more disappointed when this last-minute canceling kept happening. One time, he "forgot" to tell me about a weeklong trip he had planned for work until two days before he left! I tried to let him in on how I felt, but he invalidated and dismissed my feelings, telling me it was my problem that I couldn't handle his "crazy schedule."

I felt hurt, and Jeremy wasn't on the same team with me to help me feel better, so I also felt alone. He wasn't interested in understanding my reality or working to find solutions or respecting fair boundaries. We did not share the common goal of making each other's lives better and treating each other with respect. That is when I decided to end the relationship.

Here is how I applied the Ten Skills of Communication to ending the relationship.

1. Set Personal Goals

To end the relationship (describe).

2. Choose a Time, Place, and Platform

I knew it'd be best to choose somewhere private but in person, so we could talk rather than email or text. I decided to go over to his house because it would allow me to choose when to leave.

3. Calm Down (Enough)

I prepared what I wanted to say beforehand and practiced some breathing and grounding techniques as well.

4. Remember to Listen

I reminded myself to listen to what Jeremy wanted to say and to give this conversation my full attention.

5. State Common Goals (optional)

I used the common goal of "We both want what's best for each other," which I felt was true enough!

6. Describe

I then said, "I am ending this relationship." I didn't feel it was necessary to bring up all the times he'd let me down, as he had not been very good at accepting my reality in the past.

7. Validate (optional)

He seemed shocked, so I validated that. "This seems to have come out of nowhere for you, is that right?"

I then did some alternating between describing and validating: I offered to explain more and described the general theme of "We don't seem to have the same ideas of what makes a good partner." Again, I kept it general so there weren't specific situations to argue about. I then validated his disappointment.

8. Find Solutions (optional)

This was not really necessary. We didn't live together and didn't have any mutual friends. It could be a "clean break."

9. Offer Positive Reinforcement (optional)

I thanked Jeremy for listening.

10. Practice Self-Care (very important!)

After I got home, I called a friend to talk it over and then listened to some Taylor Swift breakup songs.

Breakups are hard and complicated! Even when you feel it's the best course of action, ending a relationship with someone in this way can still be extremely difficult. But it's worth it in the long run. My current partner shares my common goals, respects my time, and communicates a lot more clearly. I'm glad I ended a relationship that wasn't working so I could find one that is a better fit!

ENDING A RELATIONSHIP WITH A COWORKER

As an aquarium biologist, I worked closely with someone—let's call her Allison—who did not treat me well. Allison and I shared common workplace goals, and we both worked hard and wanted to take care of our animals as best as we could. However, in my reality, Allison was moody and a bully. She'd give me contradictory instructions and then get mad at me when I didn't do things as she wanted. She'd blame me for ruining her tools when she was the one who'd left them beside a saltwater tank. If she was attempting to go off caffeine or sugar, well, forget it; her moods were completely inconsistent, and I was often caught in the line of fire! There was nothing anyone could do correctly, and all my coworkers and I bore the brunt of her bad temper. At the age of twenty-three, I was in my dream job working as an aquarium biologist, but I was caught in a nightmare work situation that needed to change.

I loved the job, and I wish I'd had the skills to stand up to Allison and speak up about making changes. But, instead, I left the job without telling anyone why. I think what held me back from speaking up was that I was scared to be perceived as throwing Allison under the bus. I now know that my reality was valid! If the situation happened today, I would do things a lot differently:

1. Set Personal Goals

To tell Allison that I'm leaving and that the way she treats me is very hurtful (describe with intent to be understood).

2. Choose a Time, Place, and Platform

This is best done outside the workplace, on the phone, during the evening.

3. Calm Down (Enough)

Allison made me extremely nervous because her reactions and moods were very hard to predict. Before the call, I would take time to do some guided meditation and rehearse the conversation. Having something to fidget with while on the phone would be great to help me stay calm and on track during the conversation.

4. Remember to Listen

Listening would be a very important part of this conversation. I had a lot of pent-up resentment and hurt feelings to share, but I would need to give Allison time to process and respond.

5. State Common Goals (optional)

I don't think I would state common goals, as I would want to get straight to the point and wouldn't need to see Allison ever again after leaving the job.

6. Describe

I would be sharing new information, so describing would come first, before validation. "I wanted to let you know that I am leaving this job because I've felt hurt, bullied, and worn down by the way I've been treated."

7. Validate (optional)

If Allison were to get defensive, which is very likely, I would validate by repeating what I heard and then going back to describing

"So, your intention wasn't to make me feel that way. Unfortunately for both of us, that is how I've felt."

This is also a great step to remember the listening skills because she may validate me or even apologize! I won't know unless I give her space to respond.

8. Find Solutions (optional)

This was not a part of my personal goals, so wasn't applicable or necessary.

9. Offer Positive Reinforcement (optional)

I could thank Allison for listening, depending on how the conversation went, which might make accidental encounters in the future (which could happen because we lived in the same city) less awkward.

10. Practice Self-Care (very important!)

After the conversation, I'd probably journal and talk with a friend, seeking to have my reality validated, because I doubt that Allison would have done so for me during the conversation. I'd also probably go for a walk and process our talk.

ENDING A RELATIONSHIP WITH A FRIEND

Mary and I met at college, and the beginning of our friendship was great; we liked the same things, enjoyed the same activities, and generally got along very well. However, as we got older, our lives changed. We had less to talk about, and I noticed behaviors in her that just didn't sit well with me. She would always want to get her way (she never compromised), and she was constantly asking for favors that were never reciprocated. During the time we were friends, I drastically changed the way I ate for health reasons, and instead of being supportive, Mary would often encourage me to "just have a bite" or break my new dietary restrictions. Anytime I saw her, I felt exhausted afterward. I tried to set boundaries, but they were constantly bulldozed and disrespected. I felt at the end of my rope and had tried everything I could think of to make the friendship work, but eventually I realized it was time to end the relationship.

A year went by, and I tried to distance myself from Mary through the "slow fade." I didn't call or text her as often, and I often declined plans to hang out. I thought she'd eventually get the message or be on the same page with me. Instead, she wanted to be closer.

I could have kept going with the slow fade but decided I respected Mary as a human being enough to have an uncomfortable conversation and end our friendship. Here is how I did it:

1. Set Personal Goals

To describe that I didn't want to be friends with her anymore (with the intent that she'd understand).

2. Choose a Time, Place, and Platform

Mary had invited me over to her place to hang out, and I felt that was a good, private setting to have this conversation.

3. Calm Down (Enough)

I chose to walk over to her place so I could have time to prepare for the conversation and take some deep breaths. I also brought ice water to sip on.

4. Remember to Listen

I reminded myself to be open to Mary's reaction and not defend myself too much.

5. State Common Goals (optional)

I felt we didn't really have any at this point, so I skipped this step.

6. Describe

I said, "This friendship is not something I want to spend time or energy on anymore."

7. Validate (optional)

At first, Mary was a little defensive, and so I let her be. I validated that she didn't agree with me but that I still felt the way I felt. I stayed calm. I described a bit about how I felt like our values had changed. I kept it brief and to the point. I didn't bring up every example I had of all the instances where I felt she was pushy or disrespectful.

8. Find Solutions (optional)

Thinking about how we had quite a few mutual friends and were bound to run into each other, I said, "I hope we can be on good terms when we happen to see each other in the future."

9. Offer Positive Reinforcement (optional)

After some more talking, I thanked her for listening and understanding, and then I left.

10. Practice Self-Care (very important!)

I walked home from her house and went over the conversation in my head.

Though it was difficult, the relief I felt from giving the relationship a proper ending felt great. I felt I had upheld my own values by respecting Mary enough to give her answers and let her in on my reality. I also now didn't have to manage all her requests to hang out by coming up with excuses.

I saw Mary at a wedding a few years later, and we had a pleasant conversation. I haven't spoken to her since. I sincerely hope she's doing well; by having the conversation, I feel I gave our ten-year friendship what it was owed, gave her the explanation she needed to move on, and gained the closure we both needed to move forward.

PRACTICE MAKES ~~PERFECT~~ EASIER

Think about the relationships in your life. Who are you currently in contact with? Think of someone specific. Why are you still in a relationship with them? What common goals and values do you share?

Now think about people who have left your life. Think of someone specific. Why are you no longer in each other's lives? How did your common goals change over the course of your relationship?

You can take this a step further by asking yourself about a specific relationship that ended. How did it end? Look at the Ending Relationships Checklist in the Appendix (page 270). What aspects did you do well when this relationship ended? What might you do differently the next time you have to end a similar relationship?

As always, feel free to practice with a friend. Switch roles and see how it feels to be on the receiving end of "saying goodbye." What comes up for you? Understanding both sides of a conversation is an invaluable tool!

CONCLUSION

Ending a relationship can be difficult but is sometimes necessary. Take time to think about relationships that might be bringing you distress, and consider if ending them is the right decision. Once you are sure a relationship must end, the steps of communication will guide you toward the most peaceful, respectful, relieving conclusion.

Congratulations on taking steps toward more effective conversations and boundary-setting! Successful communication takes work, but it is well worth it.

If you're feeling a bit overwhelmed with all this new information and you're not sure where to go from here, that's okay. Please remember, there's no need to do everything at once. Start with the first skill of setting personal goals, and move slowly through the rest of the skills until they become second nature. Use (and reuse) the practice exercises to really hone each skill. Michael Jordan was not born knowing how to shoot three-pointers, or even how to dribble a basketball! If we want to get better at something, we need consistent practice (have I mentioned this enough?). While you practice, remember to use the Credit Exercise (page 128) to highlight the things you're doing well and the progress you've made!

Once you've had some good practice with the skills, you can use this book as a handy reference whenever you need conversation guidance, skipping to sections that address the particular situations you find yourself in.

Finally, one last reminder that this book is a set of suggestions, based on my experience and training as a counselor, teacher, and human. Take what you want, and discard anything else. I fully respect that you are the expert in your own life and will do what is best for you and your relationships. My goal for this book was to describe with the intent to motivate. . . . The rest is up to you!

APPENDICES

APPENDIX I. BLANK COGNITIVE MODEL

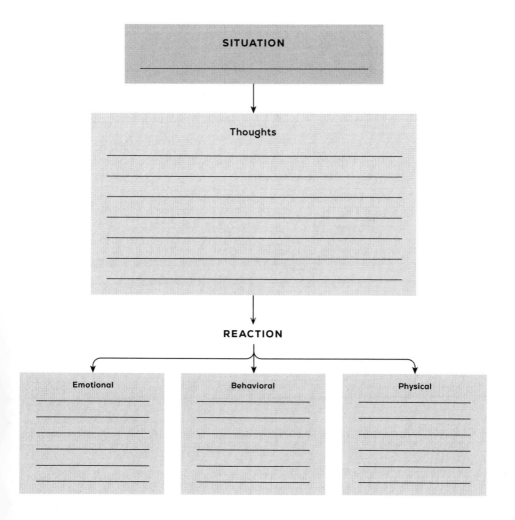

APPENDIX II. TABLE OF EMOTION WORDS

There are many theories of emotions and how to categorize them. Many clients describe how they feel and ask, "Is that an emotion?" to which I reply, "It doesn't matter!" What follows is a list of words you could use to describe your responses to a situation. If you need even more emotion words, other lists are available on the Internet.

accepted	awkward	crabby	distressed	flummoxed
admiring	beleaguered	crazed	disturbed	flustered
adored	bereaved	crazy	down	fond
affectionate	bewildered	cross	dreading	forlorn
afraid	bewitched	courageous	eager	friendly
aggravated	bitter	cruel	earnest	frightened
aggressive	blessed	defeated	easygoing	frustrated
agitated	blissful	defiant	ecstatic	fuming
agonized	blue	dejected	elated	furious
agreeable	bored	delighted	embarrassed	generous
alarmed	bummed out	dependent	emotional	glad
alienated	calculating	depressed	empty	gleeful
amazed	calm	desirous	enamored	gloating
amused	capricious	despairing	enchanted	gloomy
angry	caring	despondent	energetic	glum
anguished	cautious	determined	enraged	gratified
annoyed	charmed	devastated	enraptured	greedy
anticipatory	cheerful	disappointed	enthralled	grief-stricken
anxious	chipper	disapproving	enthusiastic	grim
apathetic	close	discontent	envious	grouchy
apprehensive	compassionate	disdainful	equanimous	grumpy
aroused	complacent	disenchanted	euphoric	guilty
ashamed	compliant	disgusted	exasperated	happy
assertive	composed	disillusioned	excited	harried
assured	conceited	disliking	exhausted	hateful
astonished	concerned	dismayed	exuberant	heartbroken
attached	confident	displeased	fascinated	heartsick
attracted	confused	dissatisfied	fatalistic	heated
awed	contemptuous	distant	fearful	helpless
awful	content	distracted	fed up	hesitant

homesick	light	perky	sardonic	thrilled
hopeful	lively	perplexed	satisfied	timid
hopeless	lonely	pessimistic	scared	tormented
horrified	longing	pitiful	scornful	torn
hostile	loving	placid	self-assured	tranquil
humiliated	low	playful	self-congratulatory	triumphant
hurt	lulled	pleasant	self-satisfied	troubled
hysterical	lustful	pleased	sentimental	trusting
indifferent	mad	powerful	serene	turned off
indignant	maddened	powerless	shameful	uncomfortable
infatuated	melancholy	proud	shocked	unhappy
inferior	merry	pushy	skeptical	upset
infuriated	miserable	quarrelsome	smug	vain
insecure	modest	queasy	somber	validated
inspired	moody	querulous	sorrowful	venal
interested	mortified	quick-witted	sorry	vengeful
introverted	mournful	quiet	spellbound	vexed
irate	naughty	quirky	spiteful	vigilant
irritated	nervous	rageful	stingy	vivacious
isolated	open	rapturous	stoic	vulnerable
jaded	optimistic	rejected	stressed	wary
jealous	ornery	relieved	subdued	wistful
jittery	outgoing	remorseful	submissive	woeful
jolly	outraged	repentant	suffering	wonderful
jovial	overjoyed	resentful	sullen	wondering
joyful	panicky	resigned	surprised	worried
jubilant	passionate	revolted	suspicious	wrathful
keen	passive	revulsion	sympathetic	zealous
kind	patient	roused	tender	zestful
laid-back	peaceful	sad	tense	
lazy	pensive	sarcastic	terrorized	

APPENDIX III. COMMUNICATION SKILLS CHECKLIST—EXTENDED VERSION

1. Set Personal Goals
   * What are my personal goals for the conversation? Why is this conversation necessary? What am I hoping to achieve?
   * Are these goals realistic, fair, and achievable? (Goals cannot be to change someone's mind!)
   * Do my goals fall under the category of "understand" or "describe"?
   * If they're "describe," do they have an added intention (to motivate and/or to be understood)?
   * How many goals do I have? Do they need to be unified with a general theme or split into separate conversations?

2. Choose a Time, Place, and Platform
   * How urgent is this conversation?
   * Are there safety concerns that need to be addressed?
   * Are there privacy concerns that need to be addressed?
   * What has been successful in the past?
   * What has been unsuccessful in the past?
   * When would be the best time for me to have this conversation?
   * When do I think would be the best time for the other person to have this conversation?
   * What type of media or location would be best for me?
   * What type of media or location do I think would be best for the other person?
   * Should I prepare the other person for this conversation?

3. Calm Down (Enough)
   * What can I do to stay calm enough to have the conversation?
   * What will I do before the conversation?
   * What can I do during the conversation?
   * How can I prepare emotionally, physically, and logistically?

4. Remember to Listen
   * How can I show the other person I am listening?
   * Do I need to remind myself not to interrupt, say "yeah, yeah" and cut them off, or any other things that may prevent effective listening?

5. State Common Goals
   * What are our shared common goals?
   * Why am I in this relationship?
   * What are things we both want?
   * Is this goal general and something I know they'd agree with?
   * Is it phrased in positive language?

6. Validate
   * Did they use an emotion word when describing?
   * Did they use nonverbal cues?
   * How did they explain the situation?
   * How might I feel if I were in their shoes?
   * How can I show them I'm listening to them?
   * If I'm unsure, what's a tentative lead I could use or a question I could ask?

7. Describe
   * Is describing needed in this situation?
   * How am I feeling?
   * What emotion words can I use?
   * How can I describe by using non-imposing language?
   * Do I need to try to be as concise as possible?
   * Do I need to prepare to listen to and validate their reaction to my description?

8. Find Solutions
   * Is this needed as part of my personal goals?
   * Restate common goals.

- Clearly state both sets of needs.
- Propose compromises, and provide ideas for solutions.
- Ask for input, work together to find compromise.
- Agree to try a new solution, be specific, and set a check-in date.
- Check in to see how it's going, then find new solutions as needed.

9. Offer Positive Reinforcement

- What did the other person do well?
- What are behaviors I'm hoping they'll do again?
- Use verbal praise.

10. Practice Self-Care

- What do I need to do logistically?
- What do I need to do physically?
- What do I need to do emotionally?
- What do I need to do spiritually?
- Give myself credit for what I did well.

APPENDIX IV. COMMUNICATION SKILLS CHECKLIST—BRIEF VERSION

1. Set Personal Goals
2. Choose a Time, Place, and Platform
3. Calm Down (Enough)
4. Remember to Listen
5. State Common Goals
6. Validate
7. Describe
8. Find Solutions
9. Offer Positive Reinforcement
10. Practice Self-Care

APPENDIX V. BOUNDARY-SETTING CHECKLIST– EXTENDED VERSION

1. Be Aware of Boundary Needs
   - Do I have consistent negative feelings (resentment, violation, frustration, sadness) when around a specific person?
   - Have I noticed repeating cycles of behavior that are causing these emotions?
   - Have my circumstances or expectations changed within a given situation or relationship?

2. Set Personal Goals
   - Find my boundaries—get specific and clear as to what they are.
   - Is my goal realistic, fair, and achievable?
   - Does my goal fit into "describe with the intent to motivate" rather than trying to control someone's behavior?

3. Choose a Time, Place, and Platform
   - If possible, try not to have the conversation in the moment the boundary is crossed.

4. Calm Down (Enough)
   - What exercises can I do to ensure I am calm enough to have this conversation?

5. Remember to Listen
   - What listening skills might I want to remind myself of?
   - Remember to let the boundary land, then listen to see how the other person takes it in.

6. State Common Goals
   - Are the goals general and something I know they'd agree with?

7. Validate
   - Validate the other person's intentions when they cross your boundary. This shuts down defense before it begins.

8. Describe
   - Use "I feel _____" statements to help avoid imposing my reality onto theirs.
   - How much, if at all, do I want to describe why I'm setting the boundary?

9. Set the Boundary
   - Use positive language if possible.
   - Frame language in terms of how the boundary can help me.

10. Offer Alternatives
    - Remember Indiana Jones, and try to think of something to fill the potential void my boundary is causing. This will help them be able to respect my boundary if they can direct that energy elsewhere.

11. State Repercussions
    - Is a repercussion necessary? If so, choose one.
    - Is the repercussion I chose realistic?
    - Explain why the repercussion will happen. This helps them not assume my intentions later.
    - Get input if I want.

12. Offer Positive Reinforcement
    - What did the other person do well that I want to encourage more of?

13. Practice Self-Care
    - What self-care strategies do I want to employ after this conversation?

14. Be Consistent
    * What might come up as resistance to my own plan? How would I cope with that?

15. Reassess
    * When do I want to schedule a check-in (either with myself or the other person) to assess how the boundary is going?
    * When I reassess, what changes, if any, need to be made?

APPENDIX VI. BOUNDARY-SETTING CHECKLIST— BRIEF VERSION

1. Be Aware of Boundary Needs
2. Set Personal Goals
3. Choose a Time, Place, and Platform
4. Calm Down (Enough)
5. Remember to Listen
6. State Common Goals
7. Validate
8. Describe
9. Set the Boundary
10. Offer Alternatives
11. State Repercussions
12. Offer Positive Reinforcement
13. Practice Self-Care
14. Be Consistent
15. Reassess

APPENDIX VII. ENDING RELATIONSHIPS CHECKLIST

1. Set Personal Goal (to end the relationship)
2. Choose a Time, Place, and Platform (very important!)
3. Calm Down (Enough)
4. Remember to Listen
5. State Common Goals (optional)
6. Describe (this comes first as there is new info being shared)
7. Validate (optional)
8. Find Solutions (optional)
9. Offer Positive Reinforcement (optional)
10. Practice Self-Care (very important!)

NOTES

1. Judith S. Beck, *Cognitive Behavior Therapy: Basics and Beyond*, 2nd ed. (New York: Guilford Press, 2011).
2. Marsha M. Linehan. *DBT Skills Training Manual*, 2nd ed. (New York: Guilford Press, 2015).
3. Beck, *Cognitive Behavior Therapy: Basics and Beyond*, 2nd ed.
4. Linehan, *DBT Skills Training Manual*, 2nd ed.
5. Linehan, *DBT Skills Training Manual*, 2nd ed.
6. For the purposes of this book, the term Positive Reinforcement means using positive, optimistic language to reinforce behaviors. This is different from in scientific conditioning, where the term Positive Reinforcement can include punishment or the use of any introduced means to reinforce behavior.
7. Linehan, *DBT Skills Training Manual*, 2nd ed.

RECOMMENDED RESOURCES

CBT RESOURCES

To learn more about CBT, visit: cares.beckinstitute.org

To find a CBT therapist, visit: cares.beckinstitute.org/get-treatment/
clinician-directory/

DBT RESOURCES

To learn more about DBT, visit: http://behavioraltech.org/resources/faqs/
dialectical-behavior-therapy-dbt/

To find a DBT therapist, visit: behavioraltech.org/resources/find-a-
therapist

EMDR RESOURCES

EMDR is a very powerful technique that I recommend if you are feeling
weighed down or blocked by past trauma.

To find an EMDR therapist in your area, visit: www.EMDRIA.org/find-
an-emdr-therapist

OTHER RESOURCES

To find a therapist in your area, visit: www.psychologytoday.com/

ACKNOWLEDGMENTS

Thank you to my parents, for providing me a "good education and a whole lotta love," as well as to Janine, Tyler, and Valentine for your ideas, support, and finger paintings.

Thank you to Steph for being the best sounding board, devil's advocate, guinea pig, friend, teammate, captain, and partner while supporting me through this process. I'm grateful for every disagreement we've had (because I've meticulously dissected each one and then used them for this book!).

Thank you to my friends for all your support, and especially to my neighbor Natasha for helping read my extremely rough drafts!

Thank you to my cat, Hamlin, for resting your head on my arm while I was trying to type. And to my dog, Huginn, for staying optimistic and ecstatic to be alive each and every day.

Thank you to my counseling colleagues. To Annie, for listening to me talk about this book (and everything else) incessantly. To Pauline, my TIR teacher, friend, and favorite pen pal. To Jess, for all the great stories and analogies, and for being the most fun consultant! To Gerry, for being a great mentor and for teaching me how to run a private practice—and, most important, for showing me the value of an *extremely extensive* self-help book library.

Thank you to the editors, marketers, artist, and everyone else who has helped me write my first book.

Manufactured by Amazon.ca
Bolton, ON